The Best of
IRISH
COOKING

The Best of
IRISH
COOKING

Alex Barker

Gill & Macmillan

Published in Ireland by
Gill & Macmillan Ltd.
Hume Avenue, Park West
Dublin 12
with associated companies throughout
the world.

www.gillmacmillan.ie

ISBN 0 7171 3419 9

All photography supplied by
Food Features

Printed in Italy

CONTENTS

STARTERS

NETTLE BROTH (below)

This unfriendly plant has some surprisingly good things to offer. It is packed not only with vitamin C and minerals but also with many other elements useful in medicine and cosmetics. When picked in early spring, the tender young shoots can be used to make this tangy, tasty and satisfying soup.

Serves 6–8

INGREDIENTS:
4 tablespoons lard or bacon fat
$1/3$ cup/1 ounce/25 grams rolled oats
2 leeks, washed and sliced
8 oz/225 g young nettle tops, thoroughly washed
12 oz/350 g potatoes, peeled and roughly diced
$3^3/4$ cups/$1^1/2$ pints/900 ml vegetable or chicken stock
$1^1/4$ cups/$1/2$ pint/300 ml milk
Salt and freshly ground black pepper

METHOD:
1 Heat the fat in a large pan and sauté the oats until they begin to turn golden at the edges.

2 Add the leeks, nettles and potatoes and fry for a few minutes more until the nettles have wilted. Then add the stock, milk and seasonings and bring to the boil.

3 Simmer for 30 minutes, stirring occasionally, until all the vegetables are tender. Check the seasonings and put the soup through a blender, if you wish. Serve the soup with warm soda bread or potato cakes (p. 75–76).

SORREL AND THYME SOUP (above)

Sorrel is not a common vegetable, but it can be found at good stores or farmers' markets, or you can grow it yourself. It is also delicious with fish. If sorrel is unobtainable, spinach makes an acceptable alternative.

Serves 4–5

INGREDIENTS:
4 tbsp butter
1 onion, roughly chopped
8 oz/225 g potatoes, peeled and roughly chopped
A few sprigs of fresh thyme
8 oz/225 g sorrel, washed and shredded
$3^3/4$ cups/$1^1/2$ pints/900 ml chicken stock
$3/4$ cup/$1/4$ pint/150 ml double cream
Salt and pepper

METHOD:

1 Heat half the butter in a large pan and sauté the onion until it is translucent.

2 Add the potatoes, half the thyme, sorrel and stock. Bring to the boil and simmer gently for about 20 minutes or until the potatoes are very soft.

3 Cool slightly, then remove the thyme sprigs and blend the soup. Pass through a sieve for an extra smooth result and return to the pan.

4 Add half the cream and the seasonings to taste and bring gently back to the boil. If the soup is still too thick, add further stock or milk and serve with a little swirl of cream and a sprig of thyme.

PEA AND HAM SOUP

A ham hock is a vital ingredient to produce the rich and unctuous flavour of this satisfying winter warmer. The meat can be removed from the hock bone and added to the soup at the last minute if you prefer a more chunky texture.

Serves 4

INGREDIENTS:
1 cup/8 oz/225 g split peas, soaked for 1–2 hours
1 small ham hock, soaked overnight or for 3–4 hours
3 sticks celery, roughly chopped
2 onions
A few bay leaves
A handful of mint leaves
1 tsp sugar
Salt and pepper
2 tbsp crispy bacon, crumbled

METHOD:

1 Place the hock in a large pan with the celery, one quartered onion, and the bay leaves. Cover with at least 4 cups/1³/4 pints/1 litre of cold water and bring to the boil. Simmer gently for about one hour.

2 Remove the hock and bay leaves. Add the drained peas, the second onion, chopped, the mint leaves and the sugar. Bring to the boil and simmer, covered, for 1–1¹/2 hours or until the peas are tender.

3 You can now blend the soup, and then sieve it

before reheating it, or simply use a potato masher to produce a thick, rough texture. Season to taste and sprinkle with the crispy bacon. Serve with oatcakes (p. 72) or soda bread (p. 76).

GAME SOUP WITH DUMPLINGS

This hearty soup is particularly welcome when the weather begins to turn cold, and can be made using one game variety or a combination of several.

Serves 6

INGREDIENTS:
4 lb (2 kg) game carcass (hare, duck, goose or pheasant), well broken up
2 tbsp butter, oil or goose fat
1 onion, chopped
2 oz/50 g braising steak (diced)
2 oz/50 g lean ham (diced)
1 carrot, chopped
1 stick celery, chopped
2–3 cloves
1 tbsp tomato purée
1 small glass of red wine
4 cups/1³/4 pints/1 litre chicken stock
Dumplings:
1 cup/4 oz/110 g flour
4 tbsp/2 oz/50 g shredded suet or grated frozen butter
A pinch of dried thyme
Salt and black pepper
A little chopped flat leaf parsley (reserve some to garnish)

METHOD:

1 Remove any remaining pieces of meat from the bones and set aside. Heat a pan or roasting tin, add the bones and toss over a high heat for a few minutes until golden all over, or roast in the oven at 425F/220C/Gas Mark 7 for 10–20 minutes or until the fat runs out.

2 Heat the butter in a large pan and fry the onion and diced beef and ham until browned. Add the bones, carrot, celery, cloves, tomato purée, wine, seasoning and stock. Bring to the boil slowly and cover.

3 Simmer the soup for about 1 hour, stirring occasionally and skimming off any fat that rises to the surface.

4 To make the dumplings, sift the flour into a mixing bowl, then mix or stir in the fat, herbs and seasonings with sufficient water to make a soft dough. Divide into 8 balls and add to the pan of soup with any reserved pieces of meat, shredded or chopped up small.

5 Simmer gently for a further 20–30 minutes until the dumplings are fluffy and the soup has slightly reduced. Check the seasonings before serving with a sprinkling of parsley.

WATERCRESS SOUP (right)

Watercress grows wild in many parts of Ireland and has for centuries been used for excellent and highly nutritious soups. Today, gathering it requires more caution: be sure it is picked from fast-running water which is unpolluted.

Serves 4

INGREDIENTS:
1 large onion, chopped
1 tbsp sunflower oil or butter
2 bunches of watercress, washed and trimmed
2$^{1}/_{2}$ cups/1 pint/600 ml chicken or vegetable stock
$^{3}/_{4}$ cup/$^{1}/_{4}$ pint/150 ml single cream
2 tsp cornflour
Salt and freshly ground black pepper
To serve:
A little thick yogurt or cream
Sprigs of watercress or mint

METHOD:
1 Soften the onion in the oil or butter in a large pan. Trim away any large stalks from the watercress, but do not chop it, then add it to the pan with the onion.

2 Cover the pan and cook the watercress for about 5 minutes until wilted. Add the stock, bring to the boil and simmer for 10–15 minutes

3 Blend or liquidize the soup thoroughly and sieve it if a smoother consistency is required. Add the cream mixed with the cornflour, and the seasonings to taste.

4 Bring the soup gently back to the boil and stir until slightly thickened. Check the seasonings, then serve with a swirl of cream and sprig of watercress or mint.

ROASTED MUSHROOMS AND SHALLOTS WITH GOAT'S CHEESE (right)

Serve this melt-in-the-mouth snack on wedges of boxty (bread made with cooked and grated raw potatoes, p.74), toasted soda bread (p.76), or Italian focaccia.

Serves 2

INGREDIENTS:
8 shallots, peeled and halved
1 lb/450 g mixed mushrooms, wiped and sliced
4 tbsp melted butter, mixed with 1 clove crushed garlic
1 tsp fresh rosemary leaves
Salt and freshly ground black pepper
A 5-oz/150-g goat's cheese, sliced up into rounds

METHOD:

1 Bring a pan of lightly salted water to the boil and cook the shallots for 5 minutes, then drain. Preheat the oven to 400F/200C/Gas Mark 6.

2 Toss the mushrooms with the drained shallots, melted garlic butter, rosemary and seasonings.

3 Arrange on a lightly oiled baking sheet and roast for 20 minutes. Place slices of goat's cheese over the mushrooms and return to the oven for 10 minutes until the cheese has browned.

4 To serve, lightly toast some thickly sliced bread, then pile on a generous amount of the mushrooms, shallots and cheese.

HERBED TROUT PÂTÉ (above)
Fishing is a major sport in Ireland, and visitors come from around the world to sample the beautiful rivers and mountain lakes that are home to salmon, brown trout and rainbow trout.

Serves 4–6

INGREDIENTS:
12 oz/350 g smoked trout, skinned and boned
6 tbsp melted butter
1 small clove of garlic
4 tbsp fromage frais or crème fraîche
1 tbsp each of finely chopped dill and parsley
1 tbsp lemon juice
Salt and freshly ground black pepper

METHOD:

1 Place all the ingredients in a food processor and blend to a smooth paste. Check the seasonings and transfer to a small pâté dish.

2 Smooth the top and cover closely with plastic film and a lid. Chill until ready to serve with toast, and use within 2–3 days.

Tip: To keep for slightly longer, heat 6 tbsp butter until bubbling. Remove the froth and pour it into a bowl, leaving the milky residue behind. Leave to cool slightly, then spoon over the pâté to completely seal the top. Chill.

GAME TERRINE WITH FOIE GRAS AND WILD MUSHROOMS (opposite)

When game is plentiful there are many more delicious recipes to try apart from roasts or casseroles. This one is a little more time-consuming but can be made a few days in advance, leaving the terrine to mature. Use duck liver, if you can't get foie gras, but don't let it become dry or overcooked.

Serves 10–12

INGREDIENTS:
The flesh of about 1^1/$_2$ lb/675 g wild duck, pheasant or partridge
About 1^1/$_2$ lb/675 g pork fillet, trimmed
Salt and ground white pepper
A good pinch of mixed spice
1 large free-range egg, beaten
6 tbsp brandy
A little goose fat or olive oil
8 oz/225 g mixed wild mushrooms, wiped and sliced
Truffle oil
1 lb/450 g goose or duck liver, well washed
^{1}/$_2$ cup of flour
Slices of fat bacon
Goose fat, pork dripping or unsalted butter

METHOD:

1 Make a smooth paste by finely mincing the game and pork meats together, adding the seasoning, mixed spice, the egg and 2–3 tbsp brandy. Mix well and chill.

2 Heat 1 tbsp oil in a pan and fry the mushrooms until tender and the liquid evaporated. Stir in a few drops of truffle oil and the seasonings and leave to cool.

3 Cut the *foie gras* or the duck's liver into thick strips, sprinkle with seasoning, and pour over the rest of the brandy.

4 Lightly brush the inside of a terrine with goose fat. Press half of the minced mixture into the base, then add the strips of liver, then the layer of mushrooms. Top with the remaining minced mixture and press down lightly to flatten the top. Cover with a layer of fat bacon.

5 Preheat the oven to 400F/200C/Gas Mark 6. Mix some flour and water to a stiff, almost pastry thickness, and use it to seal the edges of the terrine lid. Place the terrine in a roasting tin, filling it to half the depth of the terrine with warm water. Place in the oven.

6 Bake for 45–60 minutes, testing with a skewer that the meat no longer runs pink. Leave to cool under a light weight until the next day.

7 Remove any excess fat which may have been released during cooking. The pâté may be left as it is or finished off with a layer of melted goose fat or clarified butter (see previous recipe). Decorate with bay leaves and cranberries. Leave to set and chill before serving.

8 Should you wish to turn the pâté out, it may help to stand the terrine in hot water for a few seconds.

CREAMY MUSSEL SOUP

Mussels are abundant around the coasts of Ireland, just waiting to be picked when the tide goes out. There is also an increasing trade in farmed mussels, grown on ropes in sheltered bays and coastal waters which, although they are larger and appear more succulent, have a little less flavour.

Serves 4

INGREDIENTS:
1^1/$_2$ lb/675 g fresh mussels in their shells
2 tbsp butter or olive oil
1 onion, finely chopped
1 stick celery, finely chopped
2 cloves of garlic, finely chopped
^{3}/$_4$ cup/^{1}/$_4$ pint/150 ml dry white wine

1¼ cups/½ pint/300 ml good fish stock
Salt and black pepper
1 cup/8 floz/250 ml double cream
2 tbsp chopped fresh parsley

METHOD:

1 If not already cleaned, scrub the mussels in fresh running water and scrape away the hairy beards. Rinse again and drain, discarding any that are cracked or open.

2 Heat the butter in a large pan and sauté the onion, celery and garlic together until translucent. Add the wine, stock and mussels, cover tightly, and leave to bubble for about 5 minutes or until the mussels open. Discard any that don't.

3 Add the cream, seasoning to taste, and half the parsley, and simmer for another 2–3 minutes. Serve piping hot sprinkled with the rest of the parsley.

OYSTERS

Some of the best of these are grown around Ireland's shores, and include the native, which is round, small and seasonal (May to August), and the Pacific, predominant in Europe since the 1970s, and which is longer with a frilly shell and occurs all year round. Buy oysters as fresh as possible, making sure the shells are firmly shut: any that remain open when sharply tapped should be discarded. Eat on the day of purchase or store in a fridge, loosely wrapped in a damp cloth, flat shell uppermost. Fresh oysters are best eaten with lemon juice or Tabasco sauce, but they can be wrapped in bacon and lightly grilled on skewers, put in an omelette, or prepared as follows. Recipes are for 24 oysters.

OYSTERS WITH CHAMPAGNE

INGREDIENTS

2 tbsp finely chopped shallots
¾ cup/¼ pint/150 ml champagne or chablis
A pinch of salt
1 tbsp white wine vinegar
½ cup/4 oz/110 g unsalted butter, at room temperature

METHOD:

1 In a very small pan, mix the shallots, wine, salt and vinegar together. Bring to the boil and cook gently until the liquid has reduced to about 2 tablespoons.

2 Whisk in the butter in small amounts until you have a creamy sauce, adding the strained oyster liquid. Serve the oysters topped with a little of the sauce.

OYSTERS IN CREAM WITH PINK PEPPERCORNS

INGREDIENTS

½ small cucumber, peeled, seeded and diced
1 tsp bottled pink peppercorns (*baies roses*)
1 tsp ground dried pink peppercorns
A pinch of salt
1¼ cups/½ pint/300 ml double cream

METHOD

1 Shuck the oysters, straining their liquor through fine muslin into a small pan. Place the deeper half-shells of the cleaned oysters onto rock salt on plates ready to serve.

2 To the pan, add the cucumber, peppercorns, salt and cream and bring to a gentle boil. Poach the cucumber for only 1–2 minute. Remove the peppercorns.

3 Add the oysters and poach them for a couple of minutes, then spoon them back into their shells with a little cucumber and the sauce. Sprinkle with a little ground pink pepper and serve either warm or chilled.

METHOD:

1 Place the lentils in a bowl, cover them with water, and leave them to soak for a few minutes.

2 Heat the oil in a large pan and sauté the vegetables until soft. Drain the lentils well and add to the pan with the stock. Cover, bring to the boil and simmer for 20 minutes until the vegetables and lentils are tender.

3 Blend or process the soup until it is creamy smooth, sieving it if you wish, and return it to the pan. Season to taste, add a squeeze of lemon juice and the cream, and heat through. Serve topped with the croutons, black pepper and a few parsley or coriander leaves.

HERB AND ROOT SOUP (below)

Serves 4

INGREDIENTS:
1 onion, roughly chopped
2 sticks celery, roughly chopped
1 clove of garlic, chopped
2–3 tbsp oil
8 oz (225 g) roots (potatoes, carrots, parsnips or turnips, or a mixture), peeled and chopped

LENTIL, LAMB AND RED ONION SOUP (above)
A nutritious and filling main meal soup which could easily become a vegetarian favourite, too. Simply change the stock to vegetable and finish the dish with toasted nuts or seeds.

Serves 4

INGREDIENTS:
1 cup/8 oz/225 g split red lentils
2 tbsp vegetable oil
3–4 sticks celery, roughly chopped
1 white part of leek, washed and chopped
1 carrot, grated
1 parsnip, grated
1 small onion, grated
Salt and freshly ground black pepper
5 cups/2 pints/1.2 litres good lamb stock
Squeeze of lemon juice
3/4 cup/1/4 pint/150 ml double cream
To serve:
2 tbsp bread croutons
A few leaves of coriander or parsley

4 cups/1³/₄ pints/1 litre chicken or vegetable stock
Salt and black pepper
1 tbsp each fresh parsley, basil and oregano
3–4 tbsp double cream
Parsley leaves
Crisp bread croutons

METHOD:
1 Cook the onion, celery and garlic gently in the oil until soft and translucent. Add the root vegetables, stock, seasoning and herbs, bring to the boil, cover and simmer gently until they are soft (about 20 minutes).

2 Liquidize or blend the soup in a processor until smooth, then pass through a sieve for a smoother result. Return the soup to the pan and season to taste.

3 Stir in the cream just before serving and garnish with a few croutons and parsley.

GRILLED MUSSELS WITH GARLIC AND PARMESAN (left)
A delicious way to serve mussels and one that is simplicity in itself to prepare. Cook a few more than you need and serve them cold next day with mayonnaise.

Serves 4

INGREDIENTS:
2¹/₂–3 lb/1.25–1.5 kg fresh mussels
1 glass white wine or fish stock
4 tbsp butter blended with 1 crushed clove of garlic
3 tbsp dry breadcrumbs
3 tbsp Parmesan cheese, finely grated
1 tbsp finely chopped parsley

METHOD:
1 Clean the mussels thoroughly under running water, removing the beards and discarding any that are cracked or open. Heat the wine in a large pan and add the mussels. Cover with a lid and steam until all the mussels have opened, and discard any which don't.

2 When the mussels are cool enough to handle, discard the top shells and loosen the mussels from their half-shells.

3 Mix together the crumbs, cheese and parsley and sprinkle them evenly over the mussels.

4 When ready to serve, melt the garlic butter in an ovenproof serving dish, arranging the mussels in it, and place under a hot grill for a few minutes until the topping is golden brown.

CREAMY LETTUCE AND GARLIC SOUP (above)
This can be made ahead, chilled, and kept in the fridge for one or two days. It can be served warm, but do not boil the soup as it may split due to the yogurt content.

Serves 4

INGREDIENTS:
3 spring onions, trimmed
4 cloves of garlic, peeled
1 lettuce
¹/₂ cup/4 oz/110 g low fat cream cheese
1¹/₄ cups/¹/₂ pint/300 ml warm chicken stock
1¹/₄ cups/¹/₂ pint/300 ml natural yogurt
2–3 tbsp single cream
1–2 tbsp fresh lemon juice
Salt and black pepper
A few pinches of paprika
Chives, or the green part of finely chopped scallions, to garnish

15

METHOD:

1 Place the onions, garlic, lettuce, cream cheese and half the stock in a liquidizer or food processor and blend until quite smooth, gradually adding the rest of the stock.

2 Transfer to a large cold bowl and whisk in the yogurt, cream, lemon juice and seasoning to taste. Chill until required and serve with chopped chives or onions and warm crusty bread.

PICKLED HERRINGS (below)

Although not quite as popular today, herrings were once a vital part of the Irish diet, providing a welcome relief from the ubiquitous potato.

Serves 4–6

INGREDIENTS:
6 small fresh herrings
1 medium onion, thinly sliced
6–7 tbsp malt vinegar

½ tsp pickling spice
Generous pinch of salt
A few whole black peppercorns
A few whole allspice berries
2 bay leaves

METHOD:

1 Gut, scale and wash the herrings, if they have not already been done. Pat them dry and open them out on a board, skin side up. Flatten them out using the heel of your hand, pressing all the way down the back bone.

2 Turn the fish over and, using tweezers where necessary, carefully remove the backbone and all the larger bones. Cut each fish in two down its length, then roll them up, skin side out, securing them with wooden cocktail sticks.

3 Preheat the oven to 325F/170C/Gas Mark 3. Arrange the herrings so that they fit snugly into an ovenproof dish, adding the remaining ingredients plus 7 tablespoonfuls of water. The fish should be almost covered with liquid.

4 Cover tightly with aluminium foil or a lid and cook in the centre of the oven for about 40 minutes or until the flesh is tender. Allow to cool in the liquid before chilling. Serve with marinated cucumber salad, bread, or new potatoes, and a glass of Guinness.

PHEASANT AND CHESTNUT PÂTÉ (opposite)

This rich pâté is best made a couple of days before it is required to allow it to mature. Serve with French toast or home-made oatcakes (p. 72) and a glass of red wine.

Serves 8–10

INGREDIENTS:
1 pheasant, cleaned and skinned
10 oz/275 g chestnuts, cooked and peeled
1 cup/8 oz/225 g minced veal
1 cup/8 oz/225 g minced pork
½ cup/4 oz/110 g pork fat, minced
½ tsp chopped thyme
2 eggs, beaten
Salt and pepper
Thin, fatty bacon rashers, rinds removed
For the marinade:
½ bottle red wine
1 carrot, sliced

16

1 onion, sliced
3 sprigs of thyme
6 allspice berries

METHOD:
1 Put all the marinade ingredients into a glass dish. Remove the legs, wings and breasts from the pheasant. Put all the pieces into the marinade, then cover with plastic film and refrigerate for 24 hours.

2 Remove the pheasant pieces, reserving the marinade.

3 Cut the breasts into slices, cover and reserve. Strip all the other flesh from the bones and mince or process with the chestnuts, setting aside 12 whole ones.

4 Put the pheasant mixture into a bowl with the minced veal, pork, pork fat, thyme and eggs. Stir well to incorporate all the ingredients, and season well with salt and pepper.

5 Transfer the bones and reserved marinade to a saucepan, bring to the boil, and simmer for 20 minutes.

Strain, then boil again to reduce it to about 3 tablespoonfuls. Cool, then stir into the meat.

6 Preheat the oven to 350F/180C/Gas Mark 4. Using the back of a knife, stretch the bacon rashers and use them to line a 2$^1/_2$ -pint/1.5-litre loaf tin.

7 Spread one third of the minced meat in the base of the tin, put half of the breast meat and half of the reserved chestnuts on top, cover with another third of the minced mixture and continue layering until all the ingredients have been used up. Fold any remaining bacon over the top.

8 Cover with aluminium foil and stand the tin in a roasting tin filled to a depth of 1 inch (2.5 cm) with hot water. Cook for 2 hours until the pâté has shrunk away from the sides of the tin and the juices run clear. Remove from the tin. Weight the pâté down until it is cool. Cover and refrigerate until ready to serve.

9 Using a hot knife to loosen the edges, turn out the pâté and slice it thickly. Serve with Cumberland or cranberry sauce.

MEAT DISHES

BEEF STEW WITH DUMPLINGS (opposite)

An excellent family meal that can be prepared a day or two ahead, allowing the flavours to mature. In Ireland, potatoes were sometimes added instead or as well as dumplings if there was only a little meat to go round.

Serves 4

INGREDIENTS:
2 tbsp beef dripping or oil
8 oz/225 g button onions, peeled
1½ lb/675 g stewing steak, cut into cubes
2 tbsp flour
3¾ cups/1½ pints/900 ml beef stock
Salt and freshly ground black pepper
1 clove of garlic, crushed
2 sticks of celery, chopped
1 cup/8 oz/225 g each chopped carrots and turnips
1 cup/8 oz/225 g ripe tomatoes, peeled and chopped
Dumplings:
1 cup/4 oz/110 g flour
2 tsp baking powder
A good pinch of salt
2 tbsp chopped mixed herbs
4 tbsp shredded suet

METHOD:
1 Heat the fat or oil in a large saucepan and fry the onions until lightly browned. Transfer them to a plate using a slotted spoon. Fry the meat, a few pieces at a time, until brown all over, then remove.

2 Blend the flour into the remaining juices and stir with a wooden spoon until a rich brown colour develops. Remove from the heat and gradually stir in the stock, allowing it to return to the boil and thicken, stirring constantly.

3 Add the seasoning and garlic, vegetables, onions and meat. Bring to the boil, cover, and simmer for about 1½ hours.

4 Meanwhile, prepare the dumplings by mixing the flour, salt, baking powder, herbs and fat together, adding sufficient cold water to make a soft dough. With wetted hands, form into 10–12 small dumplings, which will swell on cooking.

5 Remove the lid of the casserole, check the seasonings, and add the dumplings. Bring back to the boil and allow the liquid to gently simmer while the dumplings cook. If the liquid reduces too much, add a little extra water and continue to cook until the dumplings have nearly doubled their size.

PRESSED TONGUE

For summer weekends, when there is a crowd to feed, this is a great cold cut, especially when it is set in a good jellied parsley stock.

Serves 6–8

INGREDIENTS:
1 salted calf's tongue (take a note of the weight)
1 onion, halved
1 carrot, peeled and halved
1 stick of celery, sliced into four pieces
5–6 peppercorns
4 cloves
2 or 3 bay leaves
4 tbsp chopped chives
A large bunch of parsley
1 sachet of powdered gelatine

METHOD:
1 Wash the tongue thoroughly before soaking it for 2–3 hours; if it still seems dry and hard, soak it for longer.

2 Place the tongue in a large pan with enough water to cover it. Bring to the boil and discard the water. Cover with fresh water and add the onion, carrot, bay leaves, half the chives and the stalks of the parsley.

3 Add the lid and bring to the boil. Simmer gently for 30 minutes per pound (450 g), plus another 30 minutes. At the end of the cooking time, test for tenderness by pushing the point of a knife into the thickest part of the meat; the knife should slip in easily.

4 When satisfied that it is cooked, remove the tongue from the water and leave it in a bowl of cold water until it is cool enough to handle. Then carefully slit and peel off the skin. Curl the tongue around so that it fits very snugly inside a small cake tin or soufflé dish.

5 Simmer the cooking stock until it has reduced to about 1¼ cups/½ pint/300 ml, sprinkle on the gelatine, and allow it to dissolve completely.

18

6 Chop up all the remaining parsley and add to the cooling stock along with the rest of the chives. When the stock is just beginning to thicken, stir it well and pour it over the tongue. Place a saucer with weights on the top and leave it in the fridge overnight.

7 To serve, turn the tongue carefully out of the tin. Slice and garnish it with salad leaves, and serve with Cumberland sauce, redcurrant jelly, quince preserve or pickled pears.

MINCED BEEF, CARROTS AND ONIONS

Mashed potatoes, combined with leeks or cabbage, is a feature of Irish cooking. Here it is used as a topping for a simple minced beef stew.

Serves 4–5

INGREDIENTS:
2 tbsp vegetable oil or dripping
1 large onion, finely chopped
2 cloves of garlic, crushed
1 lb/450 g minced shin of beef
1¼ cups/½ pint/300 ml good beef or ham stock
1 cup/8 oz/225 g carrots, peeled and sliced
Salt and pepper
1 lb/450 g potatoes, peeled and quartered
1 cup/8 oz/225 g leeks, well rinsed and chopped
2 tbsp butter
A little milk

METHOD:
1 Heat the fat in a pan and fry the onion and garlic until they are translucent. Add the meat and fry it until it has browned all over.

2 Add the stock, carrots and seasoning, bring to the boil, cover, and simmer gently for 20 minutes until the meat is tender. Alternatively, transfer to a casserole and cook at 350F/180C/Gas Mark 4 for about 40 minutes.

3 Meanwhile, cook the potatoes for 15 minutes. Then add the leeks and cook for a further 5 minutes until both are tender. Drain well.

4 Mash the potatoes and leeks with the butter and milk, adding the seasonings to taste.

5 Transfer the mince to an ovenproof dish and spoon

the potato mixture over the top. Increase the oven temperature to 400F/200C/Gas Mark 6 and place in the oven to brown the topping for about 10–15 minutes.

STEAK AND OYSTER PUDDING (above)

The habit of mixing steak with oysters is centuries old, and stems from the days when oysters were the food of the poor. Alternatively, the filling could be used as the basis of a pie, using a flaky pastry crust and baking it.

Serves 4–6

INGREDIENTS:
For the pastry:
2 cups/8 oz/225 g flour
2 tsp baking powder
A pinch of salt
½ cup/4 oz/110 g shredded beef suet
Approximately 4 tbsp cold water
For the filling:
1 lb/450 g lean rump or shin of beef, cubed
8–10 oysters
Salt and pepper
1 onion, finely chopped
1 clove of garlic, crushed
4 flat field mushrooms, sliced
2 tbsp chopped parsley
1 tsp grated nutmeg
2½ cups/1 pint/600 ml beef stock

METHOD:
1 Make the pastry: sift the flour with the salt and baking powder, stir in the suet and gradually add sufficient water to make a soft dough. Knead lightly.

2 Roll out the pastry on a lightly floured surface, and set aside one third.

3 Use the larger piece of pastry to line a lightly greased 2-pint/1-litre pudding basin. Mould the pastry so that it fits the sides of the basin.

4 Put the meat and oysters into a bowl. Season a few tablespoonfuls of flour with salt and pepper and toss the meats in the flour.

5 Spoon one quarter of the meat and oysters into the basin, then layer with onion, garlic, parsley and nutmeg until the basin is full and all the ingredients have been used up. Pour over the stock.

6 Roll the remaining pastry out to form a lid for the basin, dampen the edges with water, and press it down lightly over the top to seal the edges. Cover the top of the basin with a piece of aluminium foil lined with oiled greaseproof paper, making a pleat in the centre to allow for the pudding to rise. Secure with string.

7 Steam the pudding for 3–3$\frac{1}{2}$ hours if using rump steak and 4 hours for shin of beef. Top up the saucepan with boiling water during the cooking period if it shows signs of boiling dry.

8 Using a palette knife, loosen the pudding from the basin, and either turn it out onto a warmed serving plate, or serve it directly from the basin. Serve while piping hot.

SPICED BEEF (below)

Before refrigeration, salting beef was a method of preservation. It was called corned beef, the corns being the large crystals of salt used in the process. You can make a variation of this at home, which uses beef brisket, marinated for several days in a spice mixture. This also makes an excellent cold cut.

Serves 10

INGREDIENTS:
Scant 1/2 cup/3 oz/75 g soft dark-brown sugar
1 tsp each of ground cinnamon, nutmeg, cloves and
 pepper
3–3 1/2-lb/1.5-kg piece of rolled silverside, topside or
brisket

METHOD:
1 Combine the sugar and spices together and press
the mixture evenly onto the surface of the meat. Wrap
in foil and leave in a cold place for 48 hours, turning
and basting two or three times.

2 Preheat the oven to 325F/170C/Gas Mark 3. Select a
casserole dish that will hold the joint snugly. Baste the
joint once more and wrap it up closely and securely in
foil. Place it in the dish and pour on sufficient boiling
water to almost cover it. Cover tightly with a layer of
foil and a lid and cook for 3 1/2–4 hours.

3 At the end of this time the joint should be tender,
but it won't spoil if you cook it a little longer. Partly
cool the meat in the dish, then remove and carefully
unwrap it. Either baste it again with the juices while
cooling, or sprinkle it with more sugar to form a soft
crust. It can be served hot, but carves best when cold.
Serve with small baked potatoes, salads, redcurrant jelly
or Cumberland sauce and pickles.

OXTAIL BRAISED IN RED WINE (right)
*Always plan to cook oxtail 1–2 days before you want it,
when you will find it a simple matter to remove all the
excess fat before reheating and serving it.*

Serves 3–4

INGREDIENTS:
4 tbsp sunflower oil
1 oxtail (about 2 1/4 lb/1kg), cut into pieces
2 onions, sliced
4 carrots, quartered
4 sticks celery, sliced into pieces
1 1/4 cups/1/2 pint/300 ml beef stock
1 1/4 cups/1/2 pint/300 ml red wine
Bouquet garni
2 bay leaves

1 tbsp flour
8-oz/225-g can chopped tomatoes
2 tbsp chopped parsley
Salt and black pepper

METHOD:
1 Heat half the oil in a large flameproof casserole
which has a tight-fitting lid. Sauté the pieces of oxtail
until browned on all sides.

2 Preheat the oven to 325F/170C/Gas Mark 3. Add half
the onion, the pieces of carrot and celery, the stock,
wine, bouquet garni, bay leaves and seasonings. Bring
to the boil, then transfer to the oven for 1 hour.

3 Stir well, then turn down the heat to 300F/150C/Gas
Mark 2 for a further 1 1/2–2 hours, or until the meat is
meltingly tender. Allow to get cold and store in the
fridge. Next day, remove all the excess fat and reheat.

Take out the pieces of oxtail and strain the stock, discarding the vegetables.

4 Preheat the oven to 350F/180C/Gas Mark 4. In another large pan, heat the rest of the oil and fry the remaining onion, carrots and celery until golden. Stir in the flour and cook, stirring frequently until lightly browned
.

5 Gradually add the stock, a little at a time, as it thickens. Bring back to the boil, then add the tomatoes, the oxtail and seasoning to taste. Cover and cook for a further 1 hour until tender. Sprinkle with parsley and serve with baked potatoes, and carrots and swedes lightly mashed together.

TRIPE AND ONIONS (right)
People either love or loathe tripe and many even refuse to try it. The French love it and the Irish still eat it with a pint of Guinness, although not as often as in days gone by. Make sure this dish is well seasoned and add a last touch of crunchy bacon if you wish.

Serves 4

INGREDIENTS:
1½ lb/675 g dressed tripe
Bay leaves
Salt and pepper
4 tbsp butter
1½ lb/675 g onions, peeled and sliced
4 slices of fat bacon, derinded and chopped
2 cups/¾ pint/425 ml milk
½ tsp ground nutmeg
¼ tsp ground mace
¼ cup/1 oz/25 g flour
4–5 tbsp double or soured cream

METHOD:
1 Rinse the tripe, place it in a large pan, and cover it with water. Add a few bay leaves and the seasonings and simmer, covered, for about 2 hours. Remove the tripe from the pan and cut it into small pieces.

2 Heat half the butter in a medium pan and sauté the onions and bacon until translucent. Add the tripe, the milk, bay leaves, nutmeg, mace and seasonings. Cover and simmer for another hour or until the tripe is tender.

3 In another pan, melt the rest of the butter and blend in the flour. Cook the paste for a minute without browning it, then gradually blend in the strained hot milk in which the tripe was cooked, whisking to prevent lumps forming as it comes back to the boil.

4 Once the sauce has thickened, return the onions and tripe to the pan. Stir in the cream, season to taste, and serve sprinkled with more nutmeg and ground black pepper.

IRISH STEW (overleaf)
This is one of the best loved of Ireland's deliciously simple and tasty dishes. The stew consists of lamb, potatoes and onions and to be authentic, no other ingredients should be added. It is best to make it a day in advance when any fat that has risen to the top can be removed before reheating the dish in a hot oven, browning off the potatoes at the same time.

Serves 4

INGREDIENTS:
2 lb/1 kg middle neck of lamb cutlets
1½ lb/675 g potatoes, peeled and sliced

23

2 large onions, sliced
Salt and freshly ground black pepper
1 tbsp each of parsley and thyme

METHOD:
1. Layer the meat, potatoes and onions with plenty of seasoning and the herbs in a large, deep, ovenproof casserole, finishing with the sliced potato.

2. Preheat the oven to 300F/150C/Gas Mark 2. Pour on 1/2–3/4 pint/300–400 ml of water and cover with a tightly-fitting lid or greaseproof paper. Cook for at least 2 hours until the meat and potatoes are tender.

3. Increase the oven heat to brown off the potatoes at the end of the cooking time, or cool and remove the fat that has set overnight. Heat through the following day at 400F/200C/Gas Mark 6 for about 20 minutes.

LAMB AND BEAN HOT POT (right)
This recipe would originally have been made with mutton, a slightly tougher meat which is now rarely to be found, when it was cooked slowly and for a long time. The dish can be made 1–2 days ahead of eating.

Serves 4–6

INGREDIENTS:
1 1/2 lb/675 g lamb or mutton, cubed
1 tbsp vegetable oil
1 onion, chopped
2 cloves of garlic, chopped
1 tsp paprika
8 oz/225 g carrots, peeled and chopped
8 oz/225 g swede, peeled and chopped
2 oz/50 g pearl barley
1 1/4 cups/1/2 pint/300 ml beer or stock

12 oz/350 g tomatoes, peeled and chopped
12 oz/350 g soaked and cooked haricot beans (use
 canned if you prefer)
Salt and pepper
1 lb/450 g potatoes, peeled and sliced
2 tbsp butter, melted
1 tbsp chopped parsley

METHOD:
1 Heat the oil in a large pan and cook the lamb briskly
until it has browned all over. Add the onion and garlic
and cook until softened.

2 Stir in the paprika, carrots, swede and barley. Pour
over the beer, add the tomatoes and bring to the boil.
Cover and simmer for about 40 minutes.

3 Cook the sliced potatoes in boiling water for 5
minutes, then drain.

4 Preheat the oven to 325F/170C/Gas Mark 3. Add the
beans to the lamb and season to taste. Arrange the
sliced potatoes over the top and brush with butter.
Cook for one hour or until the potatoes are crisp and
golden.

5 Serve sprinkled with parsley, or cool, cover closely
and refrigerate, then reheat the next day.

HONEY-GLAZED LEG OF LAMB (above)
*Sugar and spices, rubbed into the skin of either lamb or
pork, give a beautiful colour and rich flavour to the
meats when oven-roasted.*

Serves 6

INGREDIENTS:
1 x 5-lb/2.25-kg leg of lamb
1 tbsp oil
1 tsp each of ground cinnamon, cumin, coriander,
 ginger and paprika
3 tbsp runny honey
1 tbsp flour
1¼ cups/½ pint/300 ml good lamb stock

METHOD:
1 Preheat the oven to 425F/220C/Gas Mark 7. Place the
lamb in a roasting tin and rub it all over with the oil.
Roast for 20 minutes, turning once. Reduce the heat to
375F/190C/Gas Mark 5 and cook for an hour.

2 Warm the honey and blend in the spices. Brush this evenly over the lamb. Reduce the oven temperature to 325F/160C/Gas Mark 3 and continue to cook until the lamb is tender. (Check and turn the leg occasionally to make sure it does not burn or become too brown.)

3 Transfer the lamb to a heated serving dish to rest while you make the gravy. Drain off any excess fat and then blend the flour into what is left in the roasting pan. Cook for one minute, then whisk in the stock. Simmer until smooth and thickened and serve with the lamb, roast potatoes and cabbage. Colcannon (p. 56) can be served instead of roast potatoes.

CROWN ROAST OF LAMB WITH WHISKEY GRAVY
(left)

Ireland's second national drink (no doubt a debatable point) has many uses in cooking, but it has a special affinity with lamb, especially delicious in a sauce to which it adds a hint of sweetness and a great flavour.

Serves 6

INGREDIENTS:
1 prepared crown roast of lamb
1 1/4 cups/1/2 pint/300 ml lamb stock
Mint or parsley to garnish
Stuffing:
1 cup/8 oz/225 g ready-to-eat dried apricots
3/4 cup/1/4 pint/150 ml Irish whiskey
8 oz/225 g fat bacon, rind removed
1 clove of garlic, crushed
1 cup/3 oz/75 g fresh breadcrumbs
8 oz/225 g good pork sausage meat
2 tbsp chopped fresh parsley

METHOD:
1 Chop the apricots and place them in a bowl with the whiskey. Leave to soak for 15–20 minutes to plump up.

2 Preheat the oven to 425F/220C/Gas Mark 7. Chop the bacon small and fry it in a shallow pan until the fat runs out and the bacon starts to crisp up. Stir in the garlic and fry for 1 minute.

3 Add the breadcrumbs and stir well to absorb the bacon fat. Turn into a mixing bowl and work in the sausage meat and well-drained apricots (reserve the

liquid). Form into balls about the size of walnuts, then pack them into the centre of the prepared roast. Now weigh the joint.

4 Cover the bone ends with pieces of aluminium foil or greaseproof paper and place the joint in a close-fitting roasting tin. Sprinkle the meat with the seasonings, if you wish, and roast for 25 minutes per lb/450 g, plus another 25 minutes, basting occasionally.

5 Near to the end of the cooking time, simmer the stock and the apricot-flavoured whiskey in a small pan until it has reduced by half its volume.

6 When the meat is ready, transfer it to a carving board and place to rest in a warm place. Drain off most of the fat from the roasting tin and add the whiskey stock. Simmer, scraping up the sediment in the pan, until the reduction is as you like it or thicken it with a little flour. Check the seasoning, replace the foil caps with cutlet frills and serve with the lamb and vegetables.

CRUBEENS

The Irish like their evocative name for a traditional dish of roasted pigs' trotters! They taste delicious, and if preferred the meat can be taken off the bones, chopped, and mixed with pork sausage meat to make small patties.

Serves 4 as a starter or 2 as a main course

INGREDIENTS:
2 pigs' trotters, soaked overnight in salt water
1 large onion, peeled
1 carrot, peeled
A few bay leaves
Sprig of parsley
Sprig of thyme
1/2 lemon
A few black peppercorns
Crust:
2 cups/8 oz/225 g dried white breadcrumbs
Good pinch of paprika
6 tbsp butter
To serve:
6–8 tbsp lemon vinaigrette
Chopped parsley
Wedges of lemon

METHOD:

1 Tie the trotters together or tie them between two splints with string to prevent them from curling up during cooking.

2 Place them in a large pan with the rest of the ingredients, cover with water and a lid, and simmer for 3–4 hours or until tender, spooning off any scum as the liquid comes to the boil.

3 Remove the trotters from the pan, then place them in a shallow dish under a board to keep them flat until they are quite cold. Then cut them in half lengthways.

4 Heat the oven to 450F/230C/Gas Mark 8. Mix the crumbs with the paprika. Melt the butter in a small heatproof roasting dish, dip the half-trotters in warm butter, then coat with the crumbs and return to the roasting dish with the butter.

5 Cook for 10–15 minutes until crisp and golden. Serve with a lemon vinaigrette, wedges of lemon and soda bread (p. 76).

BACON AND POTATO FRY (opposite)

It is possible to assemble a delicious and nourishing meal in no time at all using the simplest everyday ingredients from the store cupboard. Some sliced black pudding would make this a more substantial dish.

Serves: 4

INGREDIENTS:
3–4 tbsp sunflower oil
1 onion, finely chopped
6 slices of bacon, derinded and chopped
1 lb/450 g slightly undercooked small potatoes in their skins, thinly sliced
8 oz/225 g button mushrooms, wiped
12 cherry tomatoes
1 large clove of garlic, crushed (optional)
2 tbsp finely chopped parsley
Salt and black pepper

METHOD:

1 Heat 1–2 tablespoons of oil in a large frying pan. Fry the onion until just brown, adding the bacon and tossing it gently for a further 3–4 minutes. Remove with a slotted spoon to a heated dish.

2 Add another 2–3 tablespoons of oil to the pan and, when hot, add the potatoes. Sauté them gently until evenly browned, then add the mushrooms, tomatoes, garlic, half the parsley, onion and bacon. Continue cooking for a further 5–8 minutes, stirring occasionally. Sprinkle with the seasonings and the parsley and serve.

POTTED PORK

This is similar to the French rillettes in that the meat is stewed in its own fat, with flavourings, until it is tender, then mashed and stored in an earthenware pot or stone jar. A further layer of melted fat is used to seal the top and preserve it so that it can be kept for longer. This is quite fatty, so it should be served with a sharp and tangy accompaniment, such as pickled cucumbers or shallots, or a salad dressed with a red wine vinaigrette.

Serves 6–8

INGREDIENTS:
2 lb/1 kg fat pork belly or shoulder
Sea salt and ground black pepper
1 tbsp juniper berries
A few sprigs of rosemary
Vinaigrette: Mix together
4 tbsp red wine vinegar
2 shallots, peeled and finely chopped
6–8 tbsp olive oil
Chopped chervil or flat leaf parsley

METHOD:

1 Preheat the oven to 275F/140C/Gas Mark 1. Remove the bones and rind from the pork and trim off any excess fat. Rub it all over with the sea salt, then cut it into thick strips, placing it in an ovenproof earthenware pot or dish that is a snug fit.

2 Add the juniper berries, rosemary and freshly ground black pepper. Pour on about 3/4 cup/1/3 pint/150 ml of water, cover with a tight-fitting lid, and bake for about 4 hours or until the meat is tender, cooked in its own fat which has gradually melted down.

3 Pass through a sieve, allowing time for all the fat to drip through. With two forks, gently pull the meat apart to make long strands, or lightly process it in a blender, just enough to make it spreadable. Season to taste, then pack the meat into an earthenware terrine without leaving too much space at the top.

4 Top with a little extra melted fat or butter for longer storage, then chill thoroughly, covered with plastic film. When ready to serve, slice thickly and serve on a bed of crisp, dressed salad, or with the other accompaniments and chunks of fresh, warm soda bread (p. 76).

BLACK PUDDINGS WITH CREAMED LEEKS AND CARAMELIZED APPLES

This is a good mid-week dish served with plenty of creamy mashed potatoes. Regular pork sausages could be used as an alternative to the black puddings.

Serves 4

INGREDIENTS:
4 tbsp butter
6 leeks cut into 1-in/5-cm lengths
Salt and pepper
4 small black puddings
1 tart apple, peeled and sliced
A knob of butter
2 tsp brown sugar
1 lb/450 g spring greens or green cabbage
4 tbsp double cream

METHOD:
1 Melt the butter in a pan, add the leeks, cover, and cook over a low heat for 7–8 minutes until tender. Season with salt and pepper.

2 Allow the leeks to cool slightly, liquidize them, then return them to the pan.

3 Grill the black puddings for 15–20 minutes, turning them frequently until cooked through and browned.

4 Gently cook the apple in the butter and sugar and 1–2 tablespoonfuls of water until they are tender.

5 Gently reheat the leeks and stir in the cream. Serve the black puddings sliced with mashed potato, leeks and a few slices of apple.

BOILED BACON WITH CABBAGE (right)

Boiled bacon is one of the most popular of Irish family dishes. It provides something to cut at for days on end, and there is the bonus of the remaining stock, which can be used to add rich flavour to many a simple soup.

Serves: 4–6

INGREDIENTS:
3-lb/1.5-kg joint of bacon or ham (soaked overnight if smoked)
1 lb/450 g of root vegetables (carrot, turnip, onion, celery), cut into pieces
1 lb/450 g cabbage, roughly sliced
A few bay leaves
2–3 tbsp apricot jam, marmalade or mango chutney

METHOD:
1 Drain the joint, if soaked, and place it in a large pan with water to cover it. Bring to the boil, then discard the water with any scum that has formed.

2 Cover with fresh water, adding the root vegetables and bay leaves. Bring to the boil and simmer gently for 25 minutes per lb/450 g until the meat is tender.

3 Preheat the oven to 375F/190C/Gas Mark 5. Remove the bacon from the pan, saving the liquor, and when

sufficiently cool, cut away the rind and excess fat.

4 Brush the exposed fat with warmed jam and place in the oven for about 15 minutes to develop a rich glaze,

5 Meanwhile, cook the cabbage in the bacon stock, if not too salty. Serve the bacon with the vegetables, mashed potatoes topped with butter and fennel or cumin seeds, and a light gravy or a white sauce to which parsley has been added.

SAUSAGE AND POTATO SUPPER (above)
Whether you use sausages or sausage meat for this recipe doesn't really matter, but you do need a variety of potato that is floury rather than waxy

Serves 4

INGREDIENTS:
1 lb/450 g spicy sausages or sausage meat

1 large onion, chopped
1 lb/450 g peeled potatoes, roughly chopped and par-boiled for 10 minutes
1¼ cups/½ pint/300 ml chicken stock (or light beer)
Salt and pepper
8 oz/225 g canned haricot beans, drained

METHOD:
1 Skin the sausages and form the meat into 10–12 meatballs. Sauté them in a non-stick pan with the onion until it is translucent.

2 Add the potatoes, stock and seasonings and bring to the boil. Cover and simmer for 10 minutes until the potatoes are thoroughly cooked.

3 Add the beans, check the seasonings, and cook for a further 4–5 minutes until the potatoes start to disintegrate. Serve with dark-green cabbage or spinach.

POULTRY & GAME

CHICKEN, OYSTER, MUSHROOM AND BACON PIE
(below)
All these ingredients combine in a most delicious way.
Serve with mashed potatoes and fresh spinach or
buttered cabbage.

Serves 4

INGREDIENTS:
2–3 tbsp olive oil
4 chicken breasts, skinned and cut into 1-in/2.5-cm
 cubes
2 tbsp seasoned flour
$^1/_2$ cup/4 oz/110 g bacon, chopped
2 small onions, finely chopped
1 celery stalk, finely chopped
2 cloves of garlic, crushed
2 carrots, cut into strips
8 oz/225 g oyster mushrooms, quartered
$2^1/_2$ cups/1 pint/600 ml good quality white wine
$1^1/_4$ cups/$^1/_2$ pint/300 ml chicken stock
2 tbsp cornflour, slaked with a little water
Finely grated rind of 1 lemon
Salt and pepper

1 bay leaf
2 tsp chopped parsley
2 tsp chopped thyme
8 oz/225 g flaky pastry (bought)
2 tbsp milk

METHOD:
1 Heat the olive oil in a large pan. Toss the chicken in
the seasoned flour and cook it in batches until golden
brown. Remove from the pan and set aside.

2 Sauté the bacon, onions, celery, garlic and carrots for
5–7 minutes until soft. Add the mushrooms and cook
for a further 5 minutes, then remove from the pan.

3 Deglaze the pan by adding the wine and boil to
reduce it by half. Add the stock, then the slaked
cornflour, and mix to thicken. Add the lemon rind,
seasoning, bay leaf and herbs, bring to the boil, and
simmer for 5 minutes.

4 Preheat the oven to 425F/220C/Gas Mark 7.
Stir in the chicken and vegetables and spoon into a pie
dish with a funnel in the centre. Leave until cold.

5 Roll out the pastry and cover the top of the pie,
fluting the edges and brushing it with milk. Cook for
20 minutes, then reduce the temperature to
350F/180C/Gas Mark 4 for a further 20–25 minutes.
Serve immediately.

CHICKEN POT ROAST
When times were lean, the Irish housewife knew how to
take an elderly farmyard fowl and make it tender and
tasty. There it would sit, at the bottom of a large wood-
fired oven, for as long as was necessary.

Serves 6

INGREDIENTS:
1 large onion, halved
2 thick pieces of fat bacon, chopped
$3^1/_2$–4-lb/1.5–2-kg chicken or guinea fowl
1 orange, halved
2 tbsp garlic butter
$1^1/_4$ cups/$^1/_2$ pint/300ml chicken stock or cider
A few bay leaves
Salt and black pepper
2 tbsp hazelnuts, roughly chopped
1 tbsp chopped mixed herbs
1 tbsp cornflour

METHOD:

1 Preheat the oven to 325F/170C/Gas Mark 3. Place the onion and bacon inside the chicken with half the orange, divided into segments. Spread the garlic butter all over the chicken.

2 Place it in a snug-fitting roasting dish. Pour on the stock, add the bay leaves, sprinkle with the seasonings and cover with a lid. Cook for 2 hours, basting occasionally. Test with a skewer for tenderness.

3 The chicken will probably need another 30 minutes, depending on the size. At this stage, sprinkle it with the hazelnuts and the herbs and continue cooking, uncovered, until it is golden brown.

4 Transfer the chicken to a serving dish and thicken the juices if you wish by draining off as much fat as possible, then blending in the cornflour dissolved in the remaining orange juice. Allow to thicken slightly, boiling for 1 minute, then season to taste. Serve separately or poured over the chicken, served with baked potatoes and a salad.

ROAST DUCK WITH PLUMS (right)

In its uncooked state, duck is a rather fatty meat and cooking it with fruit (see also Duck with Orange and Caramelized Onions (p. 36) is the perfect way to balance it. Plums make a rich and delicious alternative.

Serves 4

INGREDIENTS:
6-lb/2.75-kg duck, ready-to-roast
1 small orange, halved
1 small red onion, halved
1–2 tbsp olive oil
Salt and black pepper
1 stick celery, chopped
A few sage leaves
1 lb/450 g plums, halved and pitted
2 tbsp butter
1¼ cups/½ pint/300ml good chicken stock
1 tbsp dark-brown sugar
1–2 tbsp brandy
2–3 tsp cornflour

METHOD:
1 Preheat the oven to 450F/230C/Gas Mark 8. Wipe the

skin of the duck clean and dry it with a kitchen towel. Place half the orange and half the onion in the cavity, then rub the skin with oil and sprinkle with seasoning.

2 Roughly cut up the remaining orange and onion and place it in the middle of a small roasting tin with the celery, sage leaves and half the plums. Place the duck on top and pour about ¾ cup/¼ pint/150 ml water into the tin.

3 Roast the duck for 30 minutes, turning the tin round once. Then baste, and reduce the heat to 400F/200C/Gas Mark 6 and continue roasting for one hour, basting twice, until the duck is cooked through and the skin is crisp.

4 Wrap the duck completely in foil and keep it warm in the oven at 325F/170C/Gas Mark 3.

5 Sieve the juices from the tin, pressing through as much of the plum flesh as possible. Set aside to cool a little and skim off as much fat as you can.

6 Fry the rest of the plums briefly in the butter, then

transfer them to a small ovenproof gratin dish and keep warm. Cut the duck into four portions and keep warm in the oven, uncovered.

7 Reheat the sauce with the stock, brandy, sugar and seasoning to taste and any juices from the duck. Thicken if you wish with a little cornflour.

8 Serve each duck portion on top of a few plums and glaze with a little of the plum sauce.

ROAST WOODCOCK
Woodcock is best at the start of the season and hung for 4–5 days undrawn. Traditionally, they are also cooked undrawn, but you can clean them in the usual way if you prefer. A fat pigeon would be a good alternative.

Serves 1

INGREDIENTS:
1 firm, plump woodcock
2 tbsp butter, softened
1 slice of fat bacon
1 slice of toasted bread
Salt and pepper
Flour

METHOD:
1 Preheat the oven to 400F/200C/Gas Mark 6. Pluck and truss the bird ready for the oven, drawing it if you prefer. Spread with butter, then wrap and tie it up in the bacon.

2 Place the piece of toast in a small roasting tin, top with the woodcock, and roast for 15–20 minutes

3 Just before the bird is ready, remove the bacon, sprinkle with flour, baste, and return to the oven to brown off.

4 Serve on the toast garnished with watercress or salad, or with a rich wine gravy if you wish.

GAME CASSEROLE WITH HERB DUMPLINGS
Rabbit or hare, game birds such as pheasant, partridge, guinea fowl and wood pigeon, are all good in a casserole. Hare can be obtained in season, while rabbit is always available fresh or frozen; it is very similar to

chicken, but slightly richer and sweeter. Hare is a dark, rich meat, very strongly flavoured.

Serves 4

INGREDIENTS:
Salt and pepper
2 lb/1 kg rabbit, hare or other game portions
4 tbsp butter
2 onions, sliced
1 tsp powdered mustard
2 sticks of celery, finely chopped
4 oz/110 g carrots, peeled and chopped
1 1/4 cups/1/2 pint/300ml chicken stock
1 glass of Marsala or sweet sherry
Salt and black pepper

METHOD:
1 Season the joints lightly. Heat the butter in a heavy-based pan and fry the meat until browned all over. Add the onions and cook until softened. Stir in the mustard and vegetables and cook for a further minute.

2 Add the stock, Marsala and seasonings to taste. Bring to the boil gently and leave to cook, covered, very slowly until the meat is tender – about 55–60 minutes. Serve with Colcannon (p. 56), champ (p. 60), or simple mashed potatoes and a green vegetables.

RABBIT IN MUSTARD SAUCE (opposite)
In the wild, rabbits are on the increase, so it is surprising that we are eating less of them. They are also obtainable as farmed meat, producing a fatter animal with more delicately flavoured, less gamy flesh.

Serves 4

INGREDIENTS:
4–8 portions of rabbit (depending on size of portions)
1 tbsp oil
4 slices bacon, roughly chopped
8 oz/225 g button mushrooms, sliced
1 onion, chopped
2 tbsp flour
2 tbsp mild mustard
A few bay leaves
2 cups/3/4 pint/425 ml chicken stock and cider mixed
3–4 tbsp double cream

METHOD:

1 If the rabbit is wild, soak it overnight or for at least 8 hours. Then drain and dry on absorbent paper.

2 Heat the oil in a large pan. Fry the bacon gently until cooked and all the fat has run out. Remove the bacon and fry the rabbit portions until sealed all over. Remove with a slotted spoon and keep warm.

3 Add the onions and mushrooms to the pan and toss in the remaining fat until just soft. Add the flour and stir gently into the vegetables until absorbed. Then stir in the stock and cider and bring slowly to the boil, stirring all the time to prevent lumps from forming.

4 When thickened slightly, return the rabbit to the pan, cover and simmer for a further 30–50 minutes or until tender.

5 Transfer the rabbit to a serving dish. Simmer the sauce, reducing it further if not sufficiently thickened, then stir in the cream and mustard and check the seasonings. Pour over the rabbit and serve with prepared vegetables and mixed or herbed rice.

DUCK WITH ORANGE AND CARAMELIZED ONIONS (right)

Wild duck is plentiful when it is in season, but for the rest of the year farmed duck, carefully cooked, can be a good alternative.

Serves 3–4

INGREDIENTS:
1 large duck, about 4–5lb/1.75–2.25kg
12–14 small onions, peeled
A few sage leaves
1 tbsp olive oil
Salt and black pepper
Juice and rind of 2 oranges
2 tbsp caster sugar
2 tbsp raisins
3–4 tbsp Cointreau or Grand Marnier

METHOD:

1 Preheat the oven to 400F/200C/Gas Mark 6. Rinse the duck and wipe it dry, then gently prick the skin all over with a fine skewer. Place 2–3 onions and some

sage leaves inside the cavity. Rub all over with olive oil and salt and place on a trivet in a large roasting tin.

2 Roast the duck for 1½–1¾ hours, basting it occasionally and draining off the excess fat as it runs out.

3 Meanwhile, spoon 1–2 tablespoonfuls of the duck fat into a frying pan and sauté the onions until they are golden and nearly tender.

4 Drain off the fat, then add the orange juice and the rind, the sugar and the raisins to the pan. Simmer gently until the liquid begins to thicken. Baste a little of it over the duck.

5 When the duck has cooked through and the juices cease to run pink, turn the oven off and baste once again with the orange sauce. Transfer to a serving dish and leave for 10 minutes.

6 Add the liqueur to the sauce and carefully ignite it with a match. When the flame has died down, simmer the sauce until slightly reduced. Check the seasonings and serve the duck with small roast potatoes and vegetables.

ROAST PHEASANT WITH POTATO BASKETS (below)

Serves 2–3

INGREDIENTS:
1 plump pheasant
Salt and black pepper
1 small lemon
1 shallot
A little butter
2 large potatoes, peeled
Oil for frying
1 cup/5 oz/150 g fresh peas, cooked

METHOD:
1 Preheat the oven to 450F/230C/Gas Mark 8. Wipe clean the pheasant, and sprinkle it with seasoning, placing half the lemon and the shallot inside. Dot with butter and squeeze the juice of the other half of the lemon over the top.

2 In a roasting tin, place the pheasant first on one breast, then the other, roasting each side for 10 minutes. Then reduce the heat to 375F/190C/Gas Mark 5. Baste and continue to roast for 30–40 minutes or until the juices run clear when a thigh is pierced.

3 Meanwhile, slice the potatoes very thinly, dry them on kitchen paper, and layer them, neatly overlapping, into buttered tartlet tins. Roast above the pheasant for 30 mins, or until tender and crisp. Turn out, brush with butter and return to the oven to brown up. Serve filled with cooked peas.

ROAST GOOSE WITH APPLES (overleaf)

Goose is generally available fresh and frozen from early November. To be sure of obtaining one, order in advance from your local butcher or supermarket.

Serves 3–4

INGREDIENTS:
1–2 tbsp walnut oil
Sprigs of rosemary and sage
4–5 lb/1.75–2.25 kg goose, defrosted if necessary
4–6 small, red-skinned apples
1 cup/8 oz/225 g mashed potatoes
A little butter
Salt and black pepper
Flour or cornflour
Cider

METHOD:
1 Preheat the oven to 400F/200C/Gas Mark 6. As the goose is a fatty bird, gently prick the skin all over without going through to the flesh. Rub a little walnut oil over the goose and season.

2 As a rough guide, allow a cooking time of 15 minutes per lb/450 g, plus 15 minutes. Roast on a trivet for 30 minutes, then turn down the heat to 350F/180C/Gas Mark 4 for the rest of the cooking time.

3 Chop the herbs, mix with the rest of the oil and brush over the goose halfway through cooking. Now drain off the excess fat and cover with foil if the bird is becoming too brown.

4 Meanwhile, core the apples, removing most of their centres. Grate, and add to the potatoes along with the butter and seasoning. Pipe back into the apple shells. Roast with the goose for the last 20–30 minutes.

THE BEST OF IRISH COOKING

5 At the end of the recommended cooking time, check that the goose is cooked by piercing a thigh with a skewer. If the juices run clear it is ready. Transfer to a carving dish and keep warm. Goose should not be overcooked as it can become dry, but do allow 10–15 minutes for it to rest before carving.

6 Drain off as much fat from the pan as possible, leaving only the juices. Add giblet stock or cider and seasoning to taste. Bring to the boil and cook until reduced to your liking or thicken with flour. Garnish the goose with the remaining sprigs of herbs and serve with the apples and any remaining potato.

Tip: Early season goose is generally not as fatty, so don't overcook it. By Christmas, you may need to remove some fat from inside the bird before roasting it and prick the skin to help release more fat during cooking.

PIGEONS WRAPPED IN BACON (right)
Pigeons are popular in Ireland, being readily available. They have a rich gamy taste that is complemented by bacon. Prosciutto, a tasty smoked bacon, is a good alternative, with added olives to give an Italian flavour.

Serves 6

INGREDIENTS:
6 pigeons, cleaned
2 bay leaves, torn into pieces
1 cup/8 oz/225 g black olives, stoned (optional)
1 large clove of garlic, peeled
12 slices of thinly sliced bacon or prosciutto
Salt and pepper
1 tbsp olive oil
1/2 bottle dry white or red wine

METHOD:
1 Divide the olives (if using) into six and place them into the cavities of the pigeons, adding a piece of bay leaf into each.

2 Rub the garlic clove over the surface of the birds. Wrap 2 slices of bacon or prosciutto around each one, securing with a cocktail stick. Season well.

3 Heat the oil in a heavy-based casserole dish and

brown the birds on all sides for about 10 minutes.

4 Pour over the wine, bring to the boil, and simmer for 15 minutes. Cover with a lid and simmer gently for 30 minutes until the birds are very tender.

5 Remove the pigeons from the casserole and, taking care not to disturb the bacon, remove the cocktail sticks. Put the birds onto a serving plate, pour over the liquor and serve.

PIGEON IN A CRUST (overleaf)
Pastry is often used to ensure that all the juices are retained when cooking less fatty types of meat or game, and to keep them moist and succulent. Of course you can eat the crust, if you wish, as it will have absorbed some of the tasty juices, but many people discard it.

Serves 4

INGREDIENTS:
4 fresh plump pigeons
Salt and black pepper
1/2 lemon
A few sprigs of thyme

4 large cloves of garlic, peeled
4 slices of fat bacon
3 cups/12 oz/350 g flour
1 tsp salt
4 tbsp lard or butter

METHOD:
1 Rinse and wipe dry the pigeons. Season the insides, adding a squeeze of lemon juice, a sprig of thyme, and a clove of garlic into each one. Place a slice of bacon over each breast. Preheat the oven to 400F/200C/Gas Mark 6.

2 Sieve the flour into a bowl with the salt. Rub in the fat, then add sufficient cold water to make a soft but not sticky dough. Roll out thinly and cut it into four pieces. Carefully wrap a piece around each bird with the seal underneath.

3 Place the pigeons in a large roasting tray and cook for 30–40 minutes, then allow to stand for 10 minutes. Serve with steamed cabbage mixed with fried bacon and a light port-flavoured gravy.

ROAST GROUSE WITH BLUEBERRIES AND OATMEAL
Try to select young grouse – which are traditionally served pink – otherwise they can be rather tough. Older birds are only suitable for braising or casseroling.

Serves 4

INGREDIENTS:
1/2 cup/4 oz/110 g butter
4 young grouse, cleaned and plucked
Freshly ground black pepper
2 cups/8 oz/225 g blueberries
1 tbsp flour
6 tbsp beef dripping, butter or olive oil
1 large onion, finely chopped
1 1/4 cups/4 oz/110 g medium oatmeal
4 tbsp crème de mûre, crème de cassis, or port
1 1/4 cups/1/2 pint/300 ml well flavoured game or
 chicken stock
Salt

METHOD:
1 Preheat the oven to 400F/200C/Gas Mark 6.

2 Melt the butter in a roasting pan and when it is foaming add the grouse, browning them on all sides. Season well with black pepper.

3 Spoon the blueberries into the cavities of the birds. Roast the grouse, breast sides down, in the preheated oven for 25 minutes, then dredge with flour and return to the oven for a further 10 minutes until just pink.

4 Scoop the blueberries from the middle of the birds and set aside. Put the birds onto a serving plate and keep hot.

5 Melt the dripping in a frying pan, add the onion and cook gently for 10 minutes until light brown. Stir in the oatmeal and cook for 5 minutes until it is toasted and crumbly.

6 Pour off any excess fat from the roasting pan and, over a medium heat, deglaze the pan with the crème de mûre or other liqueur, scraping any sediment from the bottom of the pan.

7 Mash the blueberries with a fork, add to the pan with the stock, stir well and bring to the boil. Reduce the liquid by half to about 3/4 cup/1/4 pint/150 ml. Add seasoning to taste, then strain into a sauceboat. Serve the hot grouse with the blueberry sauce, toasted oats, and green vegetables.

HARE IN GUINNESS (overleaf)
Guinness is often used in meat and game cookery as it produces a rich, sweet-sour sauce. It is excellent with other strongly flavoured meats, such as venison and pigeon.

Serves 6

INGREDIENTS:
4 tbsp butter or oil
1 small hare, portioned
2 onions, finely chopped
2 carrots, chopped
3 cloves
3 bay leaves
Salt and pepper
2 cups/3/4 pint/425 ml Guinness

2 cups/³/₄ pint/425 ml veal or beef stock
3 tbsp flour
2–3 tbsp redcurrant jelly

METHOD:
1 Heat the butter in a large pan and fry the hare portions until browned all over. Transfer to an ovenproof casserole.

2 Fry the onions and carrots until soft, then add to the casserole with the cloves, bay leaves, seasoning, Guinness and stock. Cover closely and simmer for about 2 hours or until the meat is tender.

3 Transfer the portions of hare to another dish and whisk the flour into the stock and vegetables in the pan. Bring to the boil while still whisking, then simmer, stirring occasionally until the sauce is reduced and well thickened or as you like it.

4 Stir in the jelly, check the seasoning, and return the meat to the pan. Heat through until piping hot and serve with creamed potatoes and steamed courgette slices.

BRAISED VENISON IN RED WINE (right)
Venison is readily available throughout Ireland and is enjoyed both as a roast, casserole or pot roast. It is an extremely healthy meat, being very low in fat; but care must be taken, especially when roasting it, that it is not allowed to dry out.

Serves 4

INGREDIENTS:
2–3 tbsp sunflower oil
1 large onion, thinly sliced
2 lb/1 kg piece of venison
1¹/₄ cups/¹/₂ pint/300ml veal or beef stock
³/₄ cup/¹/₄ pint/150 ml red wine
Salt and black pepper
1 large clove of garlic, crushed
2 large sprigs of rosemary
2 tbsp butter
3 tbsp flour
4 bottled sundried tomatoes, drained of oil

METHOD:
1 In a large saucepan, heat the oil and fry the onions until they are translucent. Add the venison and quickly brown it all over.

2 Add the stock, wine, seasoning, garlic and rosemary. (You can add sliced leeks, celery or other vegetables at this stage.) Bring to the boil and transfer to an ovenproof casserole dish with a lid. Cook at 350F/180C/Gas Mark 4 for 1¹/₂ hours.

3 Rub the butter and flour together to form a smooth paste or roux. About 30 minutes before the end of the cooking time, transfer the liquor to a small pan and whisk in small lumps of the roux over a medium heat. Bring to bubbling point, stirring all the time, and when the sauce has acquired the required consistency, pour it back into the pan with the venison.

4 Add the sundried tomatoes, halved, and cook for a further 30 minutes or until the meat is tender. Serve thinly carved with tagliatelle and lightly cooked shredded cabbage.

FISH

BAKED SALMON WITH HERB BUTTER

This is an easy way to cook salmon or salmon trout intended to be eaten hot. Serve with herb butter or a herb mayonnaise. Your fishmonger will be able to prepare the fish for you if you ask him beforehand and allow him sufficient time.

Serve 6–8

INGREDIENTS:
1 x 6–7-lb/2³/4–3¹/4-kg salmon (weight before
 preparation), scaled, gutted and cleaned
1 cup/8 oz/225 g butter
2 bunches of watercress
1 bunch of dill
A few sprigs of parsley
Salt and black pepper
1 lemon

METHOD:
1 Give the fish a good wash, patting it dry with kitchen paper. Slit along the length of the underside, opening the fish out, and press very firmly along the backbone.

2 Turn it over and carefully remove the backbone all in one piece and as many of the large pin bones as possible (tweezers will help). If possible, keep the head on. Preheat the oven to 350F/180C/Gas Mark 4.

3 Dot the middle of the fish with plenty of butter, sprinkle with seasoning, and add a few sprigs of herbs. Fold the fish back into its original shape, place it in the middle of a large sheet of buttered aluminium foil, and bring the edges up, folding them to form a leakproof parcel around the fish.

4 Place in the middle of the oven and bake for 15–20 minutes. Check after 15 minutes if it is not very thick around the middle, but remember that salmon is best only just cooked through.

5 In a small pan, melt the rest of the butter and add the remaining herbs, chopped, the lemon rind and juice, and the seasonings.

6 When ready to serve, carefully peel the skin from the top of the fish. Turn it over and remove the skin from the other side. Lift the whole fish carefully out of its foil parcel onto a warmed serving dish. Strain any juices into the butter pan and bubble for 1–2 minutes.

7 Serve the fish cut into sections with the hot butter, new potatoes, and a watercress garnish.

SALMON CUTLETS WITH PRAWN SAUCE (right)

Salmon, salmon trout and brown trout are all great served with this fresh prawn sauce, that makes the dish all the more delightful and delicious to eat.

Serves 4

INGREDIENTS:
4 salmon steaks
A little butter
Salt and pepper
12 oz/350 g shell-on prawns, uncooked if possible
1 shallot
Several sprigs of parsley
Juice ¹/2 lemon
1 tbsp chopped fennel or dill
1 glass of dry white wine
³/4 cup/¹/4 pint/150 ml double cream

METHOD:
1 Preheat the oven to 350F/180C/Gas Mark 4. Place the salmon on a baking tray, dot with butter, sprinkle with seasoning, and cover closely with foil.

2 Place the raw, de-veined prawns in a pan with the quartered shallot, 2–3 sprigs of parsley, the wine and the lemon juice. Bring to the boil and cook for 2–3 minutes until they change colour, when they will be cooked. (If using cooked prawns, remove the shells and continue as below.)

3 Remove the cooked prawns, peel, and return the shells to the pan. Cook the stock until reduced by half, then strain, discarding the shells.

4 While finishing the sauce, put the salmon in to bake for about 10 minutes or until just tender.

5. Add the fennel or dill, most of the rest of the parsley, chopped, and the cream to the prawn liquor, and bring it to bubbling point. Cook gently for 4–5 minutes to thicken slightly. Add the prawns, seasoning to taste, and heat through. Serve with the salmon and a selection of hot fresh vegetables.

44

METHOD:

1 Blanch the leaves in boiling water for 1–2 minutes. Drain, rinse in cold water, then dry well on kitchen paper. First line a 1-lb/450-g loaf tin with plastic film, so that the pâté will be easy to remove, then line it with the leaves, leaving sufficient to cover the top.

2 Blend the cheese with the egg, peel and oregano. Fill the spinach-lined tin with layers of fish and cheese mixture and top with the rest of the leaves. Press down firmly and cover with oiled greaseproof paper.

3 Preheat the oven to 350F/180C/Gas Mark 4. Place the terrine in a roasting tin with sufficient water to come halfway up the side. Bake for 50–60 minutes, and when cool, place it to chill in the fridge.

4 When chilled, or the next day, carefully turn out and serve with a salad and a light, orange-flavoured dressing and an orange and red onion salad.

TROUT FRIED IN OATMEAL

This is a great breakfast or supper dish which can be prepared earlier, ready to cook at the last minute. Herrings can be treated in much the same way or, if they are quite small, thoroughly cleaned but left whole and given a good coating of oatmeal.

Serves 4

INGREDIENTS:
4 trout, filleted and skinned
1 large egg
1 cup/3 oz/75 g medium oatmeal
Salt and pepper
4 tbsp butter
1 lemon

METHOD:

1 Wipe the fillets clean and dry them. Beat the egg on a shallow dish with 1–2 tablespoonfuls of water. Mix the oatmeal with the seasoning and place on another shallow dish.

2 Dip the fillets in egg, then coat them thoroughly in oatmeal. Arrange on a plate until ready to cook.

3 Heat half the butter in a non-stick frying pan and fry a few fillets at a time for 5–6 minutes, turning once half way through. Don't let the oatmeal brown too much.

SALMON AND SPINACH TERRINE (above)

Although this would appear complicated to make, it really does take only minutes to prepare and keeps moist and succulent for several days. Instead of the spinach you could use sorrel, if available.

Serves 6

INGREDIENTS:
4 oz/110 g spinach or sorrel leaves, young but not too small, washed and trimmed
5 oz/150 g soft cream cheese
1 egg, beaten
2 tsp finely grated orange rind
1 tbsp chopped oregano
1 lb 4 oz/550 g salmon or firm white fish, skinned, boned and cut into strips

46

4 When the fillets are firm, transfer them to a heated dish while cooking the others in the remaining butter. Serve with a wedge of lemon and fresh wholemeal or soda bread (p. 76).

FILLET OF SEA TROUT WITH A MEDLEY OF VEGETABLES (below)

Fresh sea trout, otherwise known as salmon trout, is one of those rare treats to be thoroughly enjoyed. Simple flavours and accompaniments are all that are required.

Serves 4

INGREDIENTS:
2 small carrots, peeled and thinly sliced
1/2 yellow pepper, diced
1 medium red onion, halved and thinly sliced
1 large tomato, deseeded, halved and sliced
Crushed black peppercorns
A few sprigs of fennel or dill
A few sprigs of parsley
2 cups/3/4 pint/425 ml good fish stock
4 sea trout fillet portions
2 tbsp dry white wine
Salt

METHOD:
1 Place the vegetables in a pan with the peppercorns, herbs and stock. Bring to the boil and cook for 5 minutes.

2 Strain off the stock and pour about 1 inch/2.5 cm of it into a frying pan. Add the fish and bring it to a gentle boil. Cover with aluminium foil and poach for about 5 minutes or until the fish is just firm.

3 Transfer the fish to a heated dish and simmer the stock, with the wine, until reduced by about half. Strain back into the vegetable pan, reheat the vegetables, and season the liquor to taste. Serve each piece of fish on top of a pile of vegetables with some of the juices poured over.

GRILLED TROUT WITH ZUCCHINI AND GARLIC BUTTER (above)

Rainbow or brown trout are ideal for grilling or barbecuing whole. They require little preparation and take only minutes to cook. However, make sure they are thoroughly scaled and well washed beforehand.

Serves 4

INGREDIENTS:
4 good-sized trout, gutted, scaled and washed
4 tbsp butter
4 tbsp olive oil
2–3 spring onions, trimmed and finely chopped
3 cloves of garlic, crushed
Salt and black pepper
1 tbsp each chopped parsley and fennel
1 tsp crushed fennel seeds
4 medium courgettes (zucchini), sliced

47

METHOD:

1 Melt the butter in a small pan with the oil, onions, garlic, seasonings, herbs and seeds. Preheat the grill, broiler or barbecue.

2 Wipe the trout inside and out, then brush all over with the herb butter. Cook for 3–4 minutes each side, brushing frequently with more butter. Allow longer if the fish are large or very thick in the middle.

3 About halfway through, add the courgettes to the rack and also brush them with herb butter. Turn once or twice and cook for only a few minutes until golden. Serve the trout and courgettes together accompanied by baked potatoes or tagliatelle.

MIXED SEAFOOD PIE (right)

It is possible to make a pie using any one fish, but several are more interesting. Include shellfish to give a depth of flavour to the dish.

Serves 4–6

INGREDIENTS:

2¹/₂ cups/1 pint/600 ml thick white sauce (method below)
Salt and pepper
2 tbsp chopped parsley and chives
8 oz/225 g squid, cleaned and cut into rings
8 oz/225 g salmon fillet, cut into small chunks
4 oz/110 g large shelled prawns
4 oz/110 g cooked shelled mussels
2 cups/1 lb/450 g mashed potatoes
A little milk or cream
A little melted butter

METHOD:

1 Make the white sauce by melting 3 tablespoonfuls of butter in a medium pan and blending in 3 tablespoonfuls of flour to make a paste. Cook for 1 minute without colouring, then gradually whisk in 2¹/₂ cups of milk. Bring back to the boil, constantly whisking or stirring with a wooden spoon to prevent lumps from forming. Cook for another 1–2 minutes.

2 When the sauce has thickened and is smooth, add seasoning to taste, half the herbs, then fold in the fish. Spoon into an ovenproof dish or several individual ramekins.

3 Preheat the oven to 375F/190C/Gas Mark 5. Mix the potato with a little milk or cream to soften it, then season with salt and pepper. Spoon it over the fish mixture and use a fork to rough up the surface. Brush with melted butter and place on a baking tray. Bake for 30–40 minutes until the top is golden.

SMOKED EEL FRITTERS WITH A SORREL SAUCE

Smoked eel is delicious simply served in a mixed fish salad, or it can be mashed and potted or made into a pâté. This more unusual combination makes a great light lunch or supper dish.

Serve 4

INGREDIENTS:
2 tbsp butter
4 oz/110 g sorrel or spinach leaves, stalks removed,

rinsed and chopped
3/4 cup/1/4 pint/150 ml fish or chicken stock
4–5 tbsp double cream
1 lb/450 g smoked eel
1 egg
1 cup/4 oz/110 g flour
1 1/4 cups/1/2 pint/300 ml milk
Salt and pepper
Oil for deep-frying

METHOD:
1 Heat the butter in a small pan and cook the sorrel gently until it has wilted. Add the stock and seasoning and leave to simmer for a few minutes.

2 Meanwhile, remove all skin and bone from the eel and break it into small pieces.

3 Whisk together the egg, flour and a little milk to make a thick, smooth paste. Gradually add the rest of the milk and whisk until smooth. Season.

4 Place about 2 inches/5 cm oil into a large lidded pan and heat until a crust of bread, when placed in the oil, turns golden in 45 seconds. Remove the bread.

5 Quickly dip the fish into the batter, draining off any excess. Put a few pieces at a time into the hot oil and cook for only 1–2 minutes, turning occasionally. When golden, drain on absorbent paper while you cook the rest.

6 Whisk or blend the sorrel sauce, then stir in the cream and season to taste. Bring back to the boil and allow to thicken slightly before serving.

COD AND POTATO CAKES WITH PARSLEY SAUCE
(right)
Creamy mashed potato mixed with flakes of firm white cod make the very best fish cakes for a simple supper or weekend brunch. Haddock can be used instead of cod.

Serves 4

INGREDIENTS:
12 oz/350 g cod, cooked, skinned and boned
2 tbsp chopped fresh parsley

1 scallion, finely chopped
Grated rind and juice of 1/2 lemon
Salt and pepper
1 1/2 cups/12 oz/350 g mashed potato
1 egg, beaten
1 1/2 cups/3 oz/75 g fine white breadcrumbs
6 tbsp butter
1–2 tbsp oil
Parsley Sauce:
1 tbsp butter
1 tbsp flour
1 1/4 cups/1/2 pint/300 ml warm milk
2 tbsp fresh parsley, finely chopped
A few drops of anchovy essence or lemon juice

METHOD:

1 Flake the fish into a bowl with the parsley, onion, lemon rind and juice, and season to taste.

2 Gently work in the potato, then shape into 8 cakes or patties. Chill well for 20 minutes.

3 Put the egg, beaten with 1 tablespoonful of cold water, in one shallow dish and the crumbs in another. Dip the cakes first in egg, then evenly coat them in the crumbs. Repeat if an extra thick coating is required.

4 Heat half the butter and the oil in a frying pan and fry 4 fish cakes at a time for about 5 minutes, turning them occasionally until they are crisp and golden. If you prefer, grill for 2–3 minutes on each side.

5 For the parsley sauce, heat the butter in a small pan and mix in the flour. Cook gently, stirring all the time, for about 2 minutes. Then gradually whisk in the milk, bringing it to the boil, still whisking, to prevent lumps from forming. Cook, stirring, for 2 minutes, then add the parsley and anchovy essence or lemon juice, seasoning to taste. Serve immediately with the fish cakes.

6 Serve the fish cakes hot with the parsley sauce and a green vegetable.

HADDOCK AND PRAWN KEDGEREE

This dish, as its name implies, originated in India at the time of the British Raj, and its popularity spread to all parts of the Empire. It was popular with the Anglo-Irish when breakfast was a more substantial affair.

Serves 6–8

INGREDIENTS:
8 oz/225 g long grain rice
Salt and black pepper
1/2 tsp ground turmeric
1 lb/450 g smoked haddock
2 hard-boiled eggs
A little butter
4 oz/110 g prawns
2/3 cup/1/4 pint/150 ml single cream
2 spring onions or chives, chopped
A generous pinch of mace

METHOD:

1 Cook the rice as directed, then add the seasoning and turmeric.

2 Poach or microwave the fish until it is just tender. Remove the skin and bones and flake the flesh. Shell and roughly chop the eggs.

3 Drain the cooked rice, then stir in the fish, eggs, a knob of butter, prawns, cream, onions and mace (or substitute a teaspoon of curry powder). Check the seasoning and serve with hot buttered toast.

HERRINGS WITH LIME AND MUSTARD SAUCE

The sharply piquant mustard sauce is an excellent foil for oily fish and would also be good with mackerel.

Serves 4

INGREDIENTS:
4 herrings, gutted, trimmed and scaled
2 tbsp flour
Salt and black pepper
3 tbsp vegetable oil
3 tbsp butter
Grated rind and juice of 2 limes (use lemons if not available)
4 tbsp olive oil
1 clove garlic, crushed
1 tsp powdered mustard
1 tbsp chopped parsley

METHOD:

1 Open the fish out on a board, skin side up, and press firmly along the backbone. Turn over and pull out the backbone in one piece with as many other bones as possible. Wipe the fish clean.

2 Mix the flour with plenty of seasoning and place it in a shallow dish. Coat the flattened fish thoroughly in the flour.

3 Heat half the oil and butter in a frying pan and cook the fish for 3–4 minutes on each side until crisp and cooked through. Transfer to a heated plate and keep warm. Continue with the rest of the fish.

4 For the sauce, mix the remaining ingredients together. Warm through and serve drizzled over the hot fish, accompanied by Colcannon (p. 56).

MONKFISH FILLETS WITH GINGER AND SOY SAUCE
(bottom of picture)
Here, oriental flavours add a touch of the exotic. Other firm-fleshed white fish can also be used in this dish.

Serves 4

INGREDIENTS:
4 fillets of monkfish or other firm fish
1/2-inch/1.5-cm piece of fresh ginger, grated
1 clove of garlic, grated
2 scallions, shredded
2 tbsp soy sauce
2 tbsp dry white wine
3 tbsp sunflower oil
Salt and pepper
To Serve:
Scallions and tomato roses

METHOD:
1 Mix together the ginger, garlic, onions, soy sauce, wine and oil. Heat gently in a frying pan, then add the fish. Cook gently, basting once or twice and turning over once.

2 When the fish is cooked through to just firm, but is still moist in the centre, serve on heated plates with spring onion tassels and tomatoes to garnish, freshly cooked noodles or rice, or sautéed potatoes.

GRILLED MACKEREL WITH GOOSEBERRIES
(top of picture)
Mackerel is plentiful in Irish waters and makes a memorable feast when eaten freshly caught and served with a lively gooseberry sauce.

Serves 4

INGREDIENTS:
4 fresh mackerel, gutted, scaled, and well washed
4 tbsp butter
Salt and black pepper
Fennel fronds
6 oz/150 g fresh gooseberries
1 tsp cornflour dissolved in 1–2 tbsp of dry white
 wine or cider vinegar
A pinch or two of sugar
To serve:
1 lemon, sliced

METHOD:
1 Pat the mackerel dry and make three diagonal slits in each side, almost through to the bone. Brush with melted butter and sprinkle generously with seasoning and a scattering of fennel.

2 Place the fish under a hot grill and cook for 3–4 minutes each side, adding more butter as necessary, until they are firm but without blackening the skin.

3 Meanwhile, heat the rest of the butter with more sprigs of fennel and cook the gooseberries until soft. Stir in the dissolved cornflour and allow to thicken, stirring all the time.

4 Pass the sauce through a sieve and return to the pan. Check the seasoning, add sugar to taste, and serve poured over the grilled mackerel, with a few fronds of fennel and segments of lemon to garnish.

2 Separate the coral from the white parts and place the scallops in a bowl, halving or quartering them if they are very large.

3 Add the lemon juice, garlic, oil, seasonings and parsley or coriander to the scallops. Move them around to coat them well.

4 Cut the bacon rashers in half, stretch them out lengthways using the back of a knife to stretch them, then roll them up into small sausages.

5 Arrange the bacon and scallop pieces alternately on the sticks and brush with any remaining marinade.

6 Preheat the grill and cook the kebabs for 3–4 minutes on each side until golden at the edges, basting them occasionally with any remaining marinade.

7 Serve the kebabs as a snack or with mashed potatoes dressed with olive oil and chopped chives or leeks, and a salad.

PAN-FRIED SCALLOPS WITH LIME (right)
Like oysters, scallops should be eaten as fresh as possible and preferably collected by divers from the bottom of the sea, which makes them more expensive. Frozen scallops are cheaper and ideal to keep but must be defrosted before cooking as they are coated in a thick layer of ice before being commercially frozen.

Serves 4

INGREDIENTS:
8–12 large fresh scallops, with or without coral
1 large juicy lime
3 tbsp olive oil
1 tbsp butter
6 oz/175g large shelled prawns
Salt and black pepper
2 tbsp chopped chives or spring onion tops

METHOD:
1 If the scallops still have their coral attached, cut them apart carefully and pat dry. Cut very large scallops into two thick slices.

2 Slice the lime very thinly. Heat a non-stick pan with the oil and butter until it begins to bubble at the edges.

SCALLOP AND BACON KEBABS (above)
Great for barbecues, the kebabs can be prepared in advance and cooked in an instant. Don't overcook, however, or the scallops will toughen.

Serves 4 for a starter or light lunch

INGREDIENTS:
8 large scallops with their coral
4 bacon rashers, rinds removed
2 tbsp lemon juice
1 clove of garlic, crushed
5–6 tbsp olive oil
Salt and pepper
1 tbsp finely chopped parsley or coriander

METHOD:
1 Soak 4 wooden saté sticks in cold water to prevent them from burning during cooking.

3 Add the lime slices first, pressing them gently to release a little of their juice, then add the scallops and toss for one minute. Add the prawns, seasoning and chives and cook for a further minute or two until the scallops have turned milky white and are just firm.

4 For a starter, serve immediately with crusty bread, or for a larger meal add rice and vegetables.

SHELLFISH SIMMERED IN CREAM (left)

A variety of shellfish are cooked together in cream with herbs and spices to produce a delicious dish for a very special occasion.

Serves 4

INGREDIENTS:
3 tbsp olive oil
1 leek, trimmed, washed and thinly sliced
1 tomato, peeled, deseeded and finely chopped
2 cloves of garlic, crushed
2 sticks of celery, finely sliced
2 bay leaves
1 tsp paprika
1 pinch of ground mace
3/4 cup/1/4 pint/150 ml good fish stock
1 lb/450 g fresh, cleaned mussels
1 1/4 cups/1/2 pint/300 ml double cream
8 oz/225 g shell-on prawns
8 scallops with coral, shelled, washed and halved
Salt and black pepper
1 tbsp whiskey or Pernod
1 tbsp chopped parsley

METHOD:
1 Heat the oil in a large pan with a lid and sauté the leek, tomato, garlic and celery until translucent.

2 Add the bay leaves, paprika, mace, fish stock and thoroughly cleaned mussels. Cover and bring to the boil, simmering for 4–5 minutes and cooking until the mussels open. Discard any that don't open and transfer the rest to a bowl with a slotted spoon.

3 Add the cream, bring to the boil and simmer for several minutes to reduce by about one third. Add the prawns and scallops, the seasoning, whiskey or Pernod and mussels, and bubble gently for 2–3 minutes until the scallops are just firm.

4 Check the seasonings and sprinkle with the parsley before serving with fresh bread.

DUBLIN BAY PRAWNS WITH GARLIC MAYO

These are in fact very small lobsters with hard shells. They are also called Norwegian lobsters and, when cooked, are better known as scampi. They keep the same

*pale, orange-pink colour even when cooked. Either
steam, poach, toss in garlic butter, or grill briefly and
serve with mayonnaise.*

Serves 4

<small>INGREDIENTS:</small>
4 tbsp butter
Juice and rind of ¹/₂ lemon
About 20 raw Dublin Bay prawns, rinsed
2 tbsp chopped fresh parsley
Salt and black pepper
Garlic mayonnaise (*aioli*)

<small>METHOD:</small>
1 Melt the butter in a large lidded saucepan with the
lemon juice and rind. When the butter is bubbling, add
the prawns, cover with the lid, and cook for about 3
minutes, shaking the pan occasionally.

2 Add the parsley and seasonings, replace the lid, and
continue to cook for another 2–3 minutes until the
prawns are just firm and the flesh has turned creamy-
pale.

3 Simply serve with garlic mayonnaise, and fresh bread
to dip into the juices.

CLAM AND POTATO POT (right)
*Clams are available for much of the year but are
usually best and more prolific in the spring. Like
mussels they need thorough cleaning and should be
eaten as fresh as possible.*

Serves 4

<small>INGREDIENTS:</small>
2 lb/1 kg clams
2 tbsp butter
1 small onion, finely diced
1 clove of garlic, crushed
Juice and rind of ¹/₂ lemon or orange
10–12 oz/275–350 g potatoes, peeled and diced
2 cups/³/₄ pint/425 ml good fish or chicken stock
Salt and black pepper
1 tbsp flat leaf parsley, chopped

<small>METHOD:</small>
1 Rinse the clams well, discarding any that are open or
cracked.

2 Heat the butter in a medium-sized saucepan and
sauté the onion and garlic together until translucent.
Add the rind and juice of the lemon, the potatoes and
the stock, then simmer for about 5 minutes or until the
potatoes are almost tender.

3 Add the clams, covering the pan and cooking them
for a further 5–6 minutes until they open up and the
potatoes are tender. Discard any clams that have not
opened.

4 When ready to serve, check the seasonings and add
the parsley, saving a little to sprinkle over the dish
before serving.

VEGETABLES

COLCANNON

This is one of Ireland's most famous dishes, also seen in Scotland. The origin of the word is uncertain but is said to come from the cannonballs used to pound vegetables.

Serves 6

INGREDIENTS:
1 lb/450 g curly kale or green cabbage, stalks removed and shredded
1 lb/450 g potatoes, cooked in their skins
8 tbsp milk or cream
1 bunch of spring onions, washed and chopped
Salt and black pepper
6–8 tbsp butter

METHOD:
1 Wash the kale, place in a pan of boiling salted water, and cook for about 10 minutes or until tender.

2 Peel the potatoes while still warm. Warm the milk through and infuse the spring onions in it.

3 Mash the potatoes well with the onions and milk to produce a soft texture, then beat in the kale and season to taste.

4 Spoon into a serving dish or individual ramekins. Make a hollow in the centre and pour in the melted butter.

POTATO AND SALMON PIE (right)

Serves 4

INGREDIENTS:
1 large onion, halved and sliced
3 sticks of celery, thinly sliced
2 cloves of garlic, crushed
2 tbsp olive oil
2 tbsp butter
1–2 oz/25–50 g smoked salmon, cut into strips
8 oz/225 g cooked fresh salmon pieces, skinned
1 tbsp chopped dill
1 lb/450 g potatoes, partly cooked and thinly sliced
5–6 tbsp double cream
1 oz/25 g grated Gruyère cheese
Salt and black pepper

METHOD:
1 Gently fry the onion, celery and garlic in oil and butter until soft but not browned.

2 Preheat the oven to 375F/190C/Gas Mark 5. Mix the smoked and cooked salmon together with the dill. Mix the cream, cheese and seasonings together.

3 Lightly grease a medium-sized ovenproof dish and make layers of the onion mixture, the salmon, and the potatoes, with spoonfuls of the cheese mixture in between. Brush with beaten egg.

4 Bake until the top is golden (about 40 minutes).

POTATO SALAD WITH SMOKED TROUT

Small potatoes, especially the waxy salad variety, are best for this dish. Leave the skins on, at least while cooking them, then peel them when cool if you prefer.

Serves 4

INGREDIENTS:
1 lb/450 g small waxy potatoes, well washed
1 tbsp butter
1 red onion, peeled and thinly sliced
5 oz/150 g mange-tout, trimmed
8 oz/225 g smoked trout fillets, skinned and flaked
5 oz/150 g baby spinach leaves
Dressing:
5 oz/150 g natural yogurt
2 tbsp creamed horseradish
Salt and black pepper
2 tbsp fresh orange juice

METHOD:
1 Halve the potatoes and cook them in lightly salted water for about 10 minutes or until just tender. Quickly drain and refresh under cold water.

2 Heat the butter in a pan and cook the onion slices until they begin to soften, but before they lose their colour. Cool.

3 Mix the cooled potatoes with the onions, peas, trout and spinach and pile into a serving bowl.

4 Mix the yogurt, horseradish, seasoning and orange juice together. Drizzle some over the salad and serve the rest separately.

SOUFFLÉD POTATOES (right)

These rich, buttery and cheesy potatoes are delicious on their own or as a luxury topping for a chicken or fish pie.

Serves 4

INGREDIENTS:
1¹/₂ lb/675 g floury potatoes
³/₄ cup/¹/₄ pint/150 ml double cream or milk
2 large free-range eggs, separated
4 tbsp butter

Salt and pepper
1 tbsp fresh tarragon, chopped
1 tsp dill seeds
1 cup/4 oz/110 g Gruyère cheese, grated

METHOD:
1 Slowly cook the unpeeled potatoes in salted water, avoiding splitting, until they are tender. Drain, dry off and peel when cool enough to handle.

2 Mash the potatoes with the cream, egg yolks and half the butter until smooth and creamy.

3 Whisk the egg whites until stiff and fold them in gently, along with the seasonings, herbs and cheese.

4 Preheat the oven to 375F/190C/Gas Mark 5. Lightly butter an ovenproof dish, spoon in the potatoes, and smooth the top. Dot the rest of the butter on the top and bake for 20–30 minutes until the top has slightly risen and is golden.

POTATO AND ONION HOT POT (above)
In Ireland, the potato is the basis of many excellent economy dishes that can be eaten simply on their own or with sausages, a bacon joint, or grilled sardines. Alternatively, they may have extra protein added to them in the form of chopped bacon or diced chicken.

Serves 4–5

INGREDIENTS:
1¹/₂ lb/675 g potatoes, thinly sliced (peeled if you wish)
3 onions, peeled and thickly sliced
2 tbsp chopped mixed fresh herbs or 2 tsp dried
Salt and black pepper
4 tbsp butter
3 oz/75 g cheese, grated
1¹/₄ cups/¹/₂ pint/300 ml milk
1¹/₄ cups/¹/₂ pint/300 ml chicken stock

METHOD:
1 Preheat the oven to 375F/190C/Gas Mark 5.

2 Layer the potatoes and onions in an ovenproof casserole, sprinkling each layer with herbs, seasoning, a few knobs of butter, and half the grated cheese.

3 Mix the milk and stock together and pour over the vegetables. Sprinkle the remaining cheese on the top

and bake for 50–60 minutes or until the potatoes are tender and the top is golden and bubbling.

ROAST POTATOES WITH HONEY AND ROSEMARY
(right)
Roast potatoes need little added because everyone loves them, but glazed with honey and spiked with rosemary they are exceedingly good to serve with ham, turkey or roast lamb.

Serves 4

INGREDIENTS:
4 tbsp goose fat or olive oil
1 lb/450 g small potatoes, peeled
Coarse sea salt
A few sprigs of rosemary
3–4 tbsp runny honey

METHOD:
1 Preheat the oven to 425F/220C/Gas Mark 7. Peel the potatoes and wipe them dry. Heat the fat or oil in a roasting tin until sizzling hot, then add the potatoes to the pan, turning them over in the hot fat until thoroughly coated. Add a sprinkling of sea salt and several small sprigs of rosemary.

2 Bake the potatoes for about 20 minutes or until part cooked through, turning and basting them in the fat once or twice. Spoon over the honey and stir around until the potatoes are well coated.

3 Continue cooking for a further 20 minutes, turning them over in the hot honey glaze once or twice. Serve when the potatoes are quite tender and a lovely brown colour.

STEAMED NEW POTATOES WITH BROCCOLI
Served hot, or cold as a spring salad, this is a colourful and crunchy way to serve potatoes.

Serves 4

INGREDIENTS:
8 small to medium new potatoes, cooked in their
 skins until just tender
8-oz/225-g piece of broccoli, split into florets and
 blanched
A little butter
2 tbsp Parmesan cheese, grated
Salt and freshly ground black pepper
Vinaigrette dressing (optional)

METHOD: (picture above left)
1 Peel the potatoes and slice them, but not too thinly. Layer on a serving plate together with the broccoli, then dot with butter and place the plate in a steamer, or over a large pan of hot water tightly covered with a lid.

2 Steam for about 5 minutes or until the vegetables are tender. Sprinkle with cheese and seasoning to taste and serve hot, or warm drizzled with a little vinaigrette dressing and the Parmesan cheese.

CHAMP (above right)
In the late 18th and early 19th centuries, the Irish poor were almost wholly dependent on potatoes as their staple food. With little meat and only the fish they could catch themselves, they became very inventive with vegetables, with the result that champ became one of the most popular ways to serve potatoes as a meal in itself. Nowadays it is usually served as a side dish to accompany simple roasts, boiled bacon or sausages.

Serves: 4

60

INGREDIENTS:
2 lb/1 kg floury potatoes
Salt and freshly ground black pepper
3/4 cup/1/4 pint/150 ml milk or buttermilk
4–5 spring onions, finely chopped
6-8 tbsp butter, melted

METHOD:
1 Cook the potatoes in their skins until tender, then allow to cool and dry. Peel, then mash well with the seasonings.

2 Heat the milk with the onions until they are tender, then gradually beat the mixture into the potatoes. The result should be a soft but not sloppy texture.

3 Serve either in 4 warmed plates or a large serving dish and make a hollow in the centre of the potatoes. Add the melted butter and serve immediately.

DUBLIN CODDLE
There seem to be numerous versions of this traditional Irish dish. It was, and still is, served on a Saturday night after the pub, or the morning after to cure a hangover! In some versions the bacon and sausages are boiled, then finished off in the oven. Sometimes, giblets and lamb chops are added to make the dish more filling. Potatoes are a recent (last century) addition but are now nearly always added.

Serves 4

INGREDIENTS:
1 lb/450 g good pork sausages
8 thick bacon rashers
2 large onions, diced
2 lb/1 kg potatoes, sliced
Salt and pepper to taste
1 1/4 cups/1/2 pint/300 ml chicken stock or dry cider
2–3 tbsp chopped parsley

METHOD:
1 Fry the sausages and bacon in a large pan until browned but not cooked through.

2 Add the onions, potatoes, seasonings and liquid. Cover tightly, bring to the boil and simmer very gently for about 1 hour or until the potatoes are cooked and the liquid has reduced.

3 Season to taste and sprinkle with parsley before serving with fresh soda bread (p.76).

FRIED PARSNIP CAKES
Serve these with grilled meats and roasts, or topped with a poached egg for a light meal. Replace the parsnips with potatoes if you prefer.

Makes 8

INGREDIENTS:
1 spring onion, finely chopped
2 cloves of garlic, crushed
8 oz/225 g each of carrots and parsnips, peeled
1 tbsp each of chopped chives and parsley
Salt and black pepper
Freshly grated nutmeg
2 tsp grated lemon rind and a little of the juice
1 small egg
Sunflower oil for frying
A little butter
Flour for coating

METHOD:
1 In a large bowl, mix the onion and garlic. Grate in the carrots and parsnips and mix well. Stir in most of the herbs, the seasonings, lemon rind and juice.

2 Blend in sufficient egg to bind the mixture without making it too wet. Shape into 8 flat, rounded patties, then coat them in flour.

3 Heat a little oil and butter in a pan and fry three or four at a time for 2–3 minutes on each side or until crisp and golden. Drain on kitchen paper and keep hot in the oven while cooking the rest. Garnish with the remaining herbs.

STUFFED BAKED ONIONS
This filling is ideal for all types of vegetables – aubergines, courgettes, tomatoes, peppers and onions. Serve hot as a vegetable course or accompaniment, or serve cold as part of a selection of cold starters.

Serves 4

INGREDIENTS:
4 large onions, peeled
3 tbsp olive oil
1 large clove of garlic, crushed

61

¼ cup/2 oz/50 g pearl barley
¼ cup/2 oz/50 g lentils
1 tsp mixed spice
1 tsp dried chopped mint
⅔ cup/4 oz/110 g raisins
Salt and black pepper
1¼ cup/½ pint/300 ml chicken or vegetable stock
½ red pepper, chopped
1 medium tomato, peeled and chopped
1 tbsp chopped fresh parsley

METHOD:

1 Cut the tops off the onions and scoop out the centres, leaving the shells intact. Chop the removed portions and place them in a small pan with one tablespoon of oil. Cook gently until tender.

2 Add the garlic, barley, lentils, spice, mint and seasonings. Fry for a few minutes, then stir in the stock. Bring to the boil, cover, and simmer for about 20 minutes or until the barley is tender and most of the liquid has been absorbed.

3 Preheat the oven to 350F/180C/Gas Mark 4. When the barley is almost tender, stir in a little more oil. Flatten the bases of the onion shells so that they stand firmly upright and arrange them snugly in a roasting tin. Fill them with the barley mixture.

4 Brush with a little oil, cover with foil, and bake for 30 minutes or until the onions are quite tender (large onions may take up to one hour). Baste with olive oil while cooking. Sprinkle with parsley before serving.

Tip: These vegetables are just as good prepared in advance and reheated when you are ready to serve them. Cover with foil and allow about 30 minutes in the centre of an oven preheated to 190C/375C/Gas Mark 5.

CREAMED LEEKS AND MUSTARD GREENS WITH HERB SAUSAGES (opposite)

Greens and leeks are the second most popular groups of vegetables in Ireland after potatoes. They are economical, versatile, nutritious, and taste wonderful with sausages, hot pots, and boiled ham.

Serves 4

INGREDIENTS:
6 leeks
4 tbsp butter
Salt and black pepper
8 plain or herb pork sausages
2 tsp mustard seed
2 tsp Dijon mustard
1 tbsp olive oil
2 generous handfuls of spring greens or green cabbage
2 tbsp double cream

METHOD:

1 Trim the leeks, wash them well, then cut them into pieces. Cook gently with the butter and seasonings until soft. Liquidize or blend them in a processor and return them to the pan.

2 Fry the sausages. In another pan, dry fry the mustard seeds until they begin to pop and burst, then mix them with the mustard and oil.

3 Remove the stalks from the greens and cook them in boiling water for 2–3 minutes or until tender. Drain them well and toss them in the mustard mixture.

4 When ready to serve, reheat the leeks, adding the cream and seasonings to taste. Serve the leeks with the sausages and the mustard greens on the side.

DESSERTS

4 Bake for 20 minutes, then reduce the heat to 350F/180C/Gas Mark 4 and bake for a further 20 minutes. Remove from the oven and allow to cool slightly before serving with custard or whipped cream.

BLACKBERRY MOUSSE (below)
The season for gathering fresh blackberries is rather short, but frozen ones are always available and so too are other soft fruits, which can be freely substituted.

Serves 4

INGREDIENTS:
1 lb/450 g blackberries or a mixture of black or red
  soft fruits, cleaned
8 tbsp caster sugar

APPLE AND BLACKBERRY PIE (above)

Serves 6–8

INGREDIENTS:
1 lb/450 g short-crust pastry (can be bought)
1 lb/450 g apples, peeled, quartered (cores removed)
1 lb/450 g blackberries, washed, with stalks removed
Generous cup/4 oz/110 g soft brown sugar
A few cloves, crushed
1 tsp ground cinnamon
1 egg white, slightly whisked
2 tbsp caster sugar

METHOD:
1 Preheat the oven to 400F/200C/Gas Mark 6. Line a large pie dish with about two thirds of the pastry, reserving the remainder for the lid.

2 Place the apples, blackberries, sugar, cloves and cinnamon into the pie dish. Cover with the remaining pastry, sealing the edges with a little water.

3 Press the pastry edges neatly together and make a hole in the centre. Brush with egg white and sprinkle with sugar.

2 large egg whites
3/4 cup/1/4 pint/150 ml whipping cream
A few mint leaves

METHOD:
1 Set aside a few berries for later. Mix the rest of the fruit in a pan with half the sugar and 2 tbsp water or fruit juice, and heat for only a few minutes until the juices run out. Press through a sieve and chill.

2 Whisk the egg whites and sugar until they are thick and glossy. Whip the cream until softly peaked, reserving a little for decoration.

3 Gently fold the cream, egg whites and fruit (keep back 2–3 tbsp) together, then spoon into serving glasses. Top with the remaining cream, fruit and fruit syrup. Chill and add a mint leaves just before serving.

BLACKCURRANT LEAF WATER ICE
Fresh young blackcurrant leaves have an intensely green scent with musky undertones which impart a subtle and unique flavour to a sorbet. Only a handful of the small young leaves are needed, so beg, borrow or steal some if you can.

Serves 4

INGREDIENTS:
10 fresh young blackcurrant leaves
2 1/2 cups/1 pint/600 ml water
Scant cup/6 oz/170 g sugar
Juice of six limes and the rind of one
1 egg white, whisked

METHOD:
1 Place the leaves, water and sugar in a pan and bring to the boil gradually, stirring as the sugar dissolves. Continue boiling until a syrup forms. Cover and leave to cool completely.

2 Strain the syrup and add the lime juice and rind. Freeze in a bowl for 1–2 hours until firm but not rock solid.

3 Turn the mixture into a food processor and blend very briefly until the mixture turns grainy. Quickly fold in the whisked egg white, whisking briefly until the mixture is light and fluffy.

4 Refreeze the mixture, whisking once before solid. Allow 15 minutes for the sorbet to soften before serving it with fresh mint, blackcurrant or geranium leaves.

ELDERFLOWER SORBET
Elderflowers are too delicious to miss and the season is so short that this is one way of prolonging it. Pick the flowers early in the morning while still fresh and moist and use them as soon as possible.

Serves 4

INGREDIENTS:
About 4 oz/110 g elderflowers, washed and stripped
 from their stalks
2 1/4 cups/1 pint/570 ml water
12 oz/350 g sugar
Finely grated rind and juice of 1 large lemon or 2 limes
 (use unwaxed fruit, well washed)
1 egg white

METHOD:
1 Place the rinsed elderflowers in a large bowl with the water and sugar. Cover, and leave to soak for 2–3 hours, stirring occasionally to help the sugar dissolve.

2 Next day, strain the flavoured sugar water into a pan and bring slowly to the boil. Boil for only 1 minute.

3 Add the grated rind and the juice from the fruit and pour into a tray in the freezer, leaving until half frozen.

4 Whisk the egg white until stiff. Turn the half-frozen mixture into a mixing bowl, then beat in the egg white using a whisk. Return to the freezer tray and repeat this process of freezing and whisking twice more.

5 Finally return to the freezer and leave to freeze completely. Before serving, allow at least 15 minutes for the sorbet to soften, then scoop small spoonfuls into tall glasses and top with mint sprigs. A splash of gin poured over makes a very good addition.

Tip: If using an ice cream machine, follow steps 1 and 2, then tip the half-frozen mixture and whisked egg whites straight into the freezer bowl and process for 10–20 minutes or as directed.

ELDERFLOWER FRITTERS (below)

It is best to pick the elderflowers early in the day, preferably before the sun is high, when the flavour will be retained. If elderflower wine is not available, use a sweetish white or muscat wine.

Serves 6

INGREDIENTS:
6 large elderflower heads, with their stalks
Vegetable oil, for deep frying
For the batter:
3/4 cup/3 oz/75 g flour
A pinch of salt
2 eggs
1 tbsp vegetable oil
6 tbsp elderflower wine, white wine, or milk
To serve:
Caster sugar
Gooseberry and mint sauce

METHOD:
1 Put all the batter ingredients into a food processor and blend until smooth. Alternatively, put the flour and

salt into a large bowl, add the eggs, and beat until smooth, gradually whisking in the oil and wine until smooth.

2 Heat the oil in a deep fryer until a small piece of bread sizzles vigorously when dropped in.

3 Hold the flowers by their stalks and dip them into the batter, one at a time. Drop them gently into the oil so that the flowers and stalks are immersed, and fry until golden.

4 Drain on kitchen paper, then arrange on a serving plate. Dredge with sugar, and serve immediately with a sauce made from cooked, sieved gooseberries with sugar, and a little chopped mint.

LEMON POSSET (right above)

This was originally a drink, made from milk curdled with wine or ale. It was sometimes thickened with egg and breadcrumbs to make a light pudding.

Serves 3–4

INGREDIENTS:
1 1/4 cups/1/2 pint/300 ml double cream
2 lemons
3 tbsp medium-dry white wine
2 egg whites
2 tbsp caster sugar, or to taste
Freshly grated nutmeg or mint sprigs

METHOD:
1 Using a zester, thinly remove the rind from one of the lemons. Reserve this to sprinkle onto the finished possets as a pretty decoration.

2 Whisk the cream until thick and almost standing in peaks. Then very gradually whisk in the juice of the other lemon and then the wine until the mixture thickens up again. (If you add the lemon juice too quickly it will curdle the cream.)

3 Whisk the egg whites with the sugar until stiff enough for meringues, then carefully fold them into the whipped cream.

4 Spoon into tall glasses and chill for 20 minutes. Serve topped with the reserved lemon rind and nutmeg.

LEMON MOUSSE TART (right)

This is very rich, so a few fresh berries to decorate the tart would not go amiss.

Serves 8–10

INGREDIENTS:
Pastry:
2 cups/8 oz/225 g flour
2 tbsp ground almonds
2 tbsp caster sugar
1/2 cup/4 oz/110 g unsalted butter, softened
Lemon mousse:
Grated rind and juice of 2 large unwaxed lemons
4 large free-range eggs, separated
6 tbsp caster sugar
1 tbsp powdered gelatine
1¼ cups/1/2 pint/300 ml whipping cream
To serve:
A few fresh berries
A little sifted icing sugar

METHOD:
1 Sift the flour into a mixing bowl, stir in the ground almonds and sugar, then blend in the soft butter. Bring together into a ball, adding 1–2 tbsp cold water, if necessary, and knead very lightly to give a smooth dough. Cover with plastic film and chill for 20 minutes.

2 Preheat the oven to 400F/200C/Gas Mark 6. On a floured surface, thinly roll out the pastry and line a loose-bottomed rectangular flan tin, 6 x 9in/13 x 23cm, or a 9-in/23-cm round one. Prick the base lightly and line with greaseproof paper and baking beans. Bake for 15 minutes, then remove the paper and beans and return to the oven for a further 10–15 minutes until crisp and golden. Allow to cool.

3 Put the lemon rind and egg yolks in a bowl. Add one third of the sugar and whisk thoroughly until the mixture becomes pale, creamy and thick.

4 Put the lemon juice into a small heatproof bowl and sprinkle on the gelatine. Leave for 5 minutes, then place over a small pan of boiling water and heat through until dissolved, stirring occasionally, or place in a microwave oven, giving it 30-second bursts, and stirring occasionally. Cool slightly, then stir the gelatine mixture into the egg yolks.

5 Whip the cream to the soft peaks stage, then fold into the lemon mixture.

6 Place two egg whites (use the rest for meringues) in a very clean bowl and whisk until stiff, gradually working in the rest of the sugar. When thick and glossy, fold into the lemon mixture until evenly blended. Pour the mixture into the pastry case.

7 Chill until set, then transfer from the flan tin to a flat platter. Sprinkle with sugar and top with the berries.

GOOSEBERRY FOOL

This is the quickest and most delicious way to serve these wonderful sharp-sweet berries. Other soft fruits (not forgetting rhubarb) can also be used to make this old-fashioned dessert.

Serves 4

INGREDIENTS:
1¹/₂ lb/675 g fresh gooseberries, topped and tailed
A few elderflowers, or 2–3 tbsp elderflower wine
4–5 tbsp caster sugar
1¹/₄ cups/¹/₂ pint/300 ml whipping cream
1¹/₄ cups/¹/₂ pint/300 ml thick, fresh custard

METHOD:
1 Cook the gooseberries with the elderflowers, or wine, and the sugar until soft. Leave to cool.

2 Gently fold the whipped cream into the gooseberries with the custard and when evenly mixed, spoon into tall glasses or serving dishes. Chill before serving.

APPLE SLICES WITH OAT TOPPING

Windfall apples are ideal for these cakes, which are so moist and delicious that they are guaranteed to disappear immediately!

Serves 6

INGREDIENTS:
2 cups/8 oz/225 g flour
2 tsp baking powder
A pinch of salt
4 tbsp butter
4 tbsp caster sugar
1¹/₂ lb/675 g cooking apples
¹/₄ tsp ground cinnamon
1 large egg
5–6 tbsp milk

Topping:
4 tbsp butter
4 tbsp demerara sugar
²/₃ cup/2 oz/50 g rolled oats

METHOD:
1 Sift the dry ingredients into a bowl and rub in the butter until the mixture resembles fine breadcrumbs. Add the sugar. Preheat the oven to 325F/170C/Gas Mark 3.

2 Peel, core and chop the apples, then stir into the dry mixture along with the cinnamon, and the egg and milk beaten together. Stir until evenly blended.

3 Line the base of a loose-bottomed rectangular or square tin and spoon in the mixture. Flatten the top.

4 Melt the butter and stir in the sugar and oats until well mixed. Spread evenly over the top of the cake and flatten down lightly. Bake for about 40 minutes, or until golden brown and firm to the touch.

5 Cool slightly in the tin and cut into sections while still warm. Serve with custard, to which a little whiskey has been added, or double cream.

RASPBERRY AND RHUBARB CRUMBLE (right)

This melt-in-the-mouth crumble is delicious whether you serve it with custard, cream or a scoop of home-made vanilla ice cream.

Serves 4–6

INGREDIENTS:

2 lb/1 kg rhubarb, washed and chopped
6 tbsp honey
A few drops of genuine vanilla extract
4 oz/110 g raspberries
8 tbsp caster sugar
1 cup/4 oz/110 g plain flour
4 tbsp butter
1/3 cup/1 oz/25 g white breadcrumbs

METHOD:

1 Preheat the oven to 375F/190C/Gas Mark 5. Wash, then slice the rhubarb into an ovenproof dish. Add the honey and vanilla extract, then sprinkle on the raspberries and half the sugar.

2 Rub the flour and butter together to a crumbly texture. Add the rest of the sugar and the breadcrumbs, mix well, then spread evenly over the fruit to cover it completely. Bake for 25–30 minutes until the top is golden brown.

CARAGEEN CREAM WITH AUTUMN FRUITS

Carageen moss, also known as Irish moss or sea moss, is a type of seaweed, harvested from the rocks along the Northern Irish coast at low tide during April, May and June. It is then dried and used in both sweet and savoury dishes as a setting agent, like agar. It is available in health food stores.

Serves 6

INGREDIENTS:

1 oz/25 g dried carageen moss
Finely grated rind of 1 lemon
2 1/2 cups/1 pint/600ml milk
1 1/4 cups/1/2 pint/300 ml double cream
1 vanilla pod, split down the middle
2–3 tbsp caster sugar
To serve:
A compote of autumn fruits (see Step 4)

METHOD:

1 Pick the carageen over, removing any grit, then soak in cold water for 10–15 minutes until soft and spongy. Drain, then rinse well in cold water.

2 Put it into a saucepan with the lemon rind, milk, cream and sugar, and simmer for 10–15 minutes until the milk begins to thicken so that it will coat the back of a spoon.

3 Strain into another bowl, then add the scraped seeds from the centre of the vanilla pod. Mix in well, add extra sugar to taste, then pour into a large wetted mould, or individual ramekins.

4 Chill well for 3–4 hours, then turn the mould out onto a serving dish. Serve with a compote of autumn fruit such as blackberries and loganberries, or dried fruits such as apricots, prunes and figs.

69

BREADS & BAKES

CHOCOLATE WHISKEY CAKE (below)
There are many types of chocolate cake but this one, well laced with Irish whiskey, is something quite special – more of a pudding than a cake!

Serves 8–10

INGREDIENTS:
3 free-range eggs
1/2 cup/4 oz/110 g soft dark-brown sugar
1/4 cup/1 oz/25 g ground almonds
3/4 cup/3 oz/75 g flour, sifted
2 tsp baking powder
1/2 cup/2 oz/50 g cocoa powder, sifted
4 tbsp unsalted butter
5–6 tbsp Irish whiskey
8 oz/225 g good quality dark chocolate
1 cup/1/2 pint/300 ml double cream
1/2 cup/2 oz/50 g icing sugar, sifted
Chocolate flakes or curls

METHOD:
1 Preheat the oven to 375F/190C/Gas Mark 5. Whisk the eggs in a large clean mixing bowl with the sugar until very thick and pale and the whisk holds a trail.

2 Gently fold in the almonds, flour and cocoa powder, then half the butter, turning the mixture over gently to avoid knocking out the air. When it is smoothly blended, spoon into an 8-in/20-cm loose-bottomed cake tin, lined in the base with greaseproof paper.

3 Bake the cake for 20–30 minutes or until it is evenly risen and just firm to the touch.

4 Cool the cake in the tin before removing and placing it on a rack. Pour 3–4 tablespoonfuls of whiskey over it, letting it soak well in. Leave to cool completely.

5 Meanwhile, prepare the chocolate coating. Melt the chocolate with the remaining butter and when smooth

stir in half the cream and the sugar, saving the rest of the cream for decoration. Mix quickly and set aside until cool but still pourable.

6 Spread the chocolate mixture all over the cold cake to give an even coating. Chill until set, then decorate with the chocolate flakes and sifted icing sugar. Serve with the remaining cream whipped with the rest of the whiskey and icing sugar to taste.

PORTER CAKE (above)

Originally made with porter, a dark-brown bitter beer weaker than Guinness, but any kind of stout or dark beer would do. Wrap the cake up immediately and try to leave it for a week to mature before cutting it.

Serves 8–10

INGREDIENTS:
2 cups/8 oz/225 g flour
2 tsp baking powder
$^1/_2$ cup/4 oz/110 g butter, softened

Generous $^1/_2$ cup/4 oz/110 g soft light-brown sugar
1 tsp mixed spice
Finely grated rind of 1 lemon
$^3/_4$ cup/$^1/_4$ pint/150 ml beer
2 eggs
2 cups/12 oz/350 g mixed dried fruit

METHOD:
1 Grease and line a deep 7-in/18-cm cake tin.

2 Preheat the oven to 325F/170C/Gas Mark 3. Put everything but the dried fruit into a large bowl and beat well for 2–3 minutes until thoroughly mixed. Then stir in the dried fruit until evenly distributed.

3 Pour the mixture into the prepared tin and bake for about 1$^1/_2$ hours until well risen and firm to the touch. Cool in the tin.

4 Then, remove the cake from the tin, wrap it in greaseproof paper, and store it for several days before cutting it.

BOILED FRUIT CAKE

Centuries ago, cakes were often made this way when they were prepared at home, then sent to cook at the local baker's. This method still produces a good result.

Serves 10–12

INGREDIENTS:
A little oil
1/2 cup/4 oz/110g butter
1 generous cup/8 oz/225 g soft light-brown sugar
1 1/4 cups/1/2 pint/300 ml water
1 lb/450 g mixed dried and glacé fruits
Finely grated rind of 1 lemon
3 cups/12oz/350g flour
1 tsp bicarbonate of soda
A pinch of salt
1 large egg

METHOD:
1 Grease and line a deep 8-in/20-cm cake tin.

2 Put the butter, sugar, water, fruits and rind in a large pan and bring them very gently to simmering point, continuing to simmer for 20 minutes. Remove from the heat and cool.

3 Preheat the oven to 350F/180C/Gas Mark 4. Sieve the dry ingredients together and stir into the cooled fruit mixture along with the beaten egg. Mix thoroughly and turn into the tin, smoothing the top with a wetted spoon.

4 Bake for 15 minutes, then reduce the heat to 325F/170C/Gas Mark 3 and bake for about 1 1/4 hours. Test by pushing a skewer into the centre to see if it comes out clean. Partly cool in the tin, then turn the cake out onto a rack and cool completely. Wrap tightly and store in an airtight tin to mature for 2–3 days.

OATCAKES (below)

These are so simple that it is well worth making them at home. Although they can be cooked on a griddle or in a heavy-based skillet, slow cooking in the oven until they are crisp is the best method.

Makes 8

INGREDIENTS:
2 1/3 cups/7 oz/200 g fine to medium oatmeal, plus extra for coating
1/2 cup/2oz/50g flour

1/2 tsp bicarbonate of soda
1/4 tsp cream of tartar
1/2 tsp salt
4 tbsp butter, dripping or bacon fat
Extra flour and oatmeal for shaping

METHOD:
1 Mix the oatmeal with the sifted flour, bicarbonate of soda, cream of tartar and salt in a mixing bowl. Make a well in the centre.

2 Melt the fat with 3–4 tbsp water until bubbling, then pour it into the centre of the bowl and mix well.

3 Sprinkle a work surface with a very little flour and oatmeal. Knead the dough for 1–2 minutes, then roll it out to form a thin 9-in/23-cm circle. Cut into 8 segments and sprinkle all surfaces with more oats.

4 Transfer carefully to a baking tray and cook in an oven preheated to 350F/180C/Gas Mark 4, for 40–50 minutes until very crisp but not coloured. Leave in the oven to cool, then place on a rack to go cold. Store in an airtight tin until required.

HONEY AND OAT COOKIES (right)
The oats give these cookies a deliciously light, crumbly texture. They can be made as large or as small as you wish.

Makes about 18

INGREDIENTS:
3/4 cup/6oz/170 g butter
8 tbsp caster sugar
1 tsp ground cinnamon, nutmeg or mixed spice
1 generous cup/5 oz/150 g flour
1 tsp baking powder
1 2/3 cups/5 oz/150 g porridge oats
2 tbsp clear honey

METHOD:
1 Preheat the oven to 350F/180C/Gas Mark 4. Line two large baking trays with non-stick baking paper.

2 Cream together the butter and sugar until light and fluffy. Sift in the spices, flour and baking powder and mix well.

3 Work in the oats and honey and knead well until a ball forms. Take small pieces of dough about the size of a walnut and roll them into balls. Set them well apart on the baking trays and press them down lightly with a fork or spoon.

4 Bake for 20 minutes until the cookies have spread out and are a pale golden colour. Transfer to a cooling rack to cool completely.

RICH SHORTBREAD (overleaf, left)
Serve as an accompaniment to a dessert of strawberries and cream. Shortbread can be cooked in one large round, or as small round or finger biscuits.

Serves 6–8

INGREDIENTS:
1 1/2 cups/6 oz/170 g flour, sifted
1/2 cup/2 oz/50 g rice flour or ground rice

6 tbsp caster sugar
5 oz/150 g butter, at room temperature
Sugar for dusting

METHOD:
1 Blend the flour with the rice flour or ground rice.
Add half the sugar to the flour mixture, then rub in the
butter until the mixture resembles very fine
breadcrumbs

2 Stir in the rest of the sugar. Knead well but lightly
until the ingredients bind together. Press into
shortbread moulds or carefully roll out between sheets
of greaseproof paper. Using a cutter, shape into rounds.

3 Preheat the oven to 300F/150C/Gas Mark 2. Leave to
rest for at least 15 minutes before turning the
shortbreads onto a well buttered baking tray. Bake for
20–25 minutes, then carefully lift them onto a wire rack
to cool.

4 When completely cold, store in an airtight tin away
from other biscuits until needed. Dust liberally with
sugar before serving, if liked.

BOXTY (above)
*Boxty is made almost entirely from potatoes, both
cooked and raw. It can be made either into bread, farls
(baps), or thick pancakes. This version is best served
warm with fried bacon and eggs, or black pudding.*

Serves 4

INGREDIENTS:
8 oz/225 g raw, peeled potatoes
8 oz/225 g cooked potatoes, mashed
1/2 cup/2 oz/50 g flour
Pinch of salt

METHOD:
1 Grate the raw potato onto a plate or board covered
with absorbent paper, then blot with more paper so
that all the liquid is absorbed.

2 As soon as possible, place the grated potato into a
bowl and add the mashed potato, flour and salt, and
mix gently to a pliable dough.

3 Turn out onto a lightly floured surface and roll or
press out to form a 7–8-in/18–20-cm circle. Transfer to
a hot, lightly greased skillet or griddle and cook over a
moderate heat for 5–8 minutes.

4 When the underside is lightly browned, carefully turn
it over and cook the other side. Continue to turn, if
you wish, until golden brown and cooked through.
Serve piping hot, split through the middle and

74

buttered, or reheat for breakfast and serve with bacon, eggs, sausages or black pudding.

POTATO CAKES

These are soft and scone-like and are delicious for breakfast, supper, or as part of a light lunch. Top with scrambled eggs, crumbled bacon, smoked trout and crème fraîche, smoked salmon with sour cream, or rare roast beef with a creamy horseradish sauce.

Serves 4

INGREDIENTS:
8 oz/225 g potatoes cooked in their jackets then peeled
2 tbsp melted butter
1/2 cup/2 oz/50 g flour
Salt and pepper

METHOD:
1 Pass the potatoes through a potato ricer, then gently mix them with the butter, flour and seasonings.

2 Turn the dough onto a lightly floured surface, rolling it out to about a 1/2-inch/11/2-cm thickness. Cut into 4 quarters, triangles or squares.

3 Heat a griddle or heavy-based frying pan dusted with flour, until the flour begins to colour. Add the potato cakes and cook for a few minutes until lightly browned on both sides. Serve immediately, or cool and reheat as required.

BARM BRACK (below)

This fruity yeast loaf is traditionally served on Halloween when it would have had rings hidden in it to predict marriage before Easter for the lucky recipient. However, it makes a great tea-time treat all-year-round.

Makes 2 loaves

INGREDIENTS:
5 cups/11/4 lb/560 g strong bread flour
A pinch of salt
1 tsp mixed spice
4 tbsp butter
1 cup/6 oz/170g sultanas or chopped dates
4 tbsp candied peel, finely chopped

4 tbsp caster sugar
2 large free-range eggs
1/2 sachet dried ready-to-use yeast
1 1/4 cups/1/2 pint/300 ml tepid water
Topping:
2 tbsp runny honey, warmed

METHOD:
1 Sift the dry ingredients into a large mixing bowl. Rub in the butter to form a crumbly texture, then stir in the fruits and sugar.

2 Beat the eggs together, then blend the yeast into the water. Stir both into the dry ingredients and mix with a wooden spoon so that it all comes together to a stiff paste.

3 Beat or stir hard for a few minutes, then divide between two lightly greased and floured 1-lb/450-g loaf tins. Leave in a warm place until the loaves have doubled their size.

4 Preheat the oven to 400F/200C/Gas Mark 6. Bake the loaves for 30–40 minutes until well risen and golden, spreading them with the warmed honey just before the end of the cooking time.

RICH TEA BRACK (right)
Although very similar to Barm Brack, this is not made with yeast and contains larger amounts of fruits and spices.

Serves 8–10

INGREDIENTS:
1 lb/450 g mixed dried fruit
2 tbsp candied peel
1 generous cup/8 oz/225 g soft light-brown sugar
1 2/3 cups/14 fl oz/400 ml black tea, warm
3 cups/12 oz/350 g flour
2 tsp baking powder
2 tsp mixed spice
2 large free-range eggs, beaten
1 tbsp honey or golden syrup to glaze

METHOD:
1 Grease and line 2 x 1-lb/.5-kg loaf tins. Put the fruit and sugar into a large bowl and pour on the tea. Leave for 24 hours, if possible.

2 Preheat the oven to 325F/160C/Gas Mark 3. Sift the dry ingredients into a large bowl, then gradually work in the beaten egg and the soaked fruits until well amalgamated.

3 Spoon into the tins and bake for about 1 1/2 hours or until firm to the touch. Ten minutes before the end of cooking, brush the tops with the honey to glaze and return to the oven for a further few minutes.

4 Partly cool in the tins, then turn out and cool on a wire rack. Wrap tightly and store for 1–2 days to mature before cutting. Serve sliced and buttered or toasted.

SODA BREAD (right)
Historically, the Irish only grew a soft wheat which was not suitable for the yeast breads so common elsewhere. Hence, they developed their own breads, using bicarbonate of soda as the main raising agent and buttermilk to help it work and add flavour. These are simple, quick-to-make breads, slightly heavier than we are used to, but delicious for all that. They are good with soups and stews, with cheese and pâtés, or generously buttered fresh from the oven.

Makes 1 x 1-lb/450-g loaf or 6 farls

INGREDIENTS:
4 cups/1 lb/450g flour

1 tsp bicarbonate of soda
1 tsp salt
2 tbsp caster sugar
2 cups/³/₄ pint/425 ml buttermilk
Knob of butter

METHOD:

1 Preheat the oven to 400F/200C/Gas Mark 6. Sift the dry ingredients into a large bowl. Make a well in the centre and stir in the buttermilk. Mix very lightly with a knife to produce a soft dough.

2 Butter a baking tray. Lightly form the dough into a circle, place onto the tray and shape into a neat circle, leaving the surface rough. (Handle the mixture as little as possible for the best results.) Sprinkle with more flour, then cut a cross on the top, dividing the bread into quarters.

3 Bake for 30 minutes, then reduce the heat to 325F/170C/Gas Mark 3 until pale golden, well risen, and crusty on top. Cover with a clean cloth and leave to cool.

SODA FARLS

These individual chunks of soda bread can be cooked either in the oven or on a griddle. They are delicious warm, split and buttered and filled with bacon, sausages, fried eggs or other breakfast favourites.

INGREDIENTS and METHOD as for soda bread. Makes 6 .

1 Knead the dough very lightly until smooth, then form into a circle no more than 1/2–1-in/2–2.5-cm thick (even thinner if cooking on a griddle). Cut into 6 sections.

2 Butter a baking tray and heat it in the oven at the same temperature as above. Place the pieces of dough flat on the tray and bake for about 40–45 minutes until they are well risen and golden brown. Wrap in a clean cloth to keep hot before serving.

3 To cook on a griddle or heavy cast-iron frying pan, preheat the pan until a light dusting of flour turns light brown within a few minutes. Clean and lightly butter it.

4 Place the farls in the pan and cook until risen and golden, allowing about 8–10 minutes on each side. When cooked, they should sound hollow when tapped.

CURRANT SODA BREAD

INGREDIENTS and METHOD as for soda bread. Makes 1 loaf or 6 farls.

Rub 2 tbsp butter into the dry mixture, then add 1 cup/6 oz/170 g currants or raisins to the dough while mixing in the buttermilk. Continue as above and, when cooked, wrap in a clean cloth while cooling. Serve either sliced with butter or toasted.

WHEATEN SODA BREAD

This is a variation on the soda bread theme that can be as rough textured as you like, according to the grains you use. Add more wholemeal flour, even medium oatmeal, and less white flour if you want a really coarse result.

Makes 1 loaf

INGREDIENTS:
3 cups/12 oz/350 g stone-ground wholemeal flour
1 cup/4 oz/110 g white flour
1 tsp salt
1 tsp bicarbonate of soda
2 tbsp caster sugar
4 tbsp butter
2 cups/3/4 pint/425 ml buttermilk

METHOD:
1. Put the dry ingredients into a large bowl and rub in the butter. Make a well in the centre and stir in the buttermilk. Mix lightly with a knife to produce a soft pliable dough.

2 Preheat the oven to 400F/200C/Gas Mark 6. Butter a baking tray, then lightly form the dough into a circle. Put it onto the tray and shape it into a neat circle, leaving the surface rough. Then cut a cross on the top, dividing it into quarters. Sprinkle with more flour.

3 Bake for 30 minutes, then reduce the heat to 325F/170C/Gas Mark 3 until pale golden, well risen, and crusty on top. Cover and leave to cool.

BUTTERMILK SCONES

Makes about 24 scones

INGREDIENTS:
4 cups/1 lb/450 g flour
2 tsp bicarbonate of soda
2 tsp cream of tartar
1/2 tsp salt
4–6 tbsp butter or margarine
1 1/4 cups/1/2 pint/300 ml buttermilk
Extra milk to glaze (optional)

METHOD:
1 Sift all the dry ingredients into a large bowl and lightly rub in the fat.

2 Stir in all the milk and mix to a springy dough.

3 Turn out onto a lightly floured surface and knead briefly until smooth, then roll out until the dough is 1/2–3/4-inches/1.5–2-cm thick.

4 Preheat the oven to 425F/220C/Gas Mark 7. With a 2-inch/5-cm cutter, cut out as many scones as possible, place them on lightly floured baking trays, and brush them with milk.

5 Bake for about 10 minutes until well risen and a pale golden colour.

IRISH TREACLE LOAF

Serves 8

INGREDIENTS:
4 tbsp butter
5 tbsp water

1 heaped tbsp black treacle
4 tbsp soft brown sugar
1 large egg
2 cups/8 oz/225 g flour
1/2 tsp each of mixed spice and ground ginger
1 tsp bicarbonate of soda
4 tbsp each of currants and raisins

METHOD:
1 Put the butter and water in a pan and leave on a low heat to melt. Preheat the oven to 350F/180C/Gas Mark 4.

2 Meanwhile, in a large mixing bowl, beat together the treacle, sugar and egg.

3 Sift in the dry ingredients, then add the dried fruit and melted liquid. Mix gently until well blended, then tip into a greased 1-lb/450-g loaf tin.

4 Bake for 1¼–1½ hours until firm to the touch. Partly cool in the tin before transferring to a cooling rack. Serve sliced with butter or toasted and sprinkled with caster sugar to serve with fruit compotes.

DROP SCONES (right)
So-called as the batter is literally dropped onto the griddle and cooks in a matter of minutes. They are ideal for the hungry hoards who can't wait another minute to eat!

Makes about 20

INGREDIENTS:
1½ cups/6 oz/170 g flour, sieved
A pinch of salt
1 tbsp caster sugar
2 eggs
2/3 cup/¼ pint/150 ml milk
2 tsp cream of tartar
1–2 drops of genuine vanilla extract
Oil for frying

METHOD:
1 Mix together the flour, salt and sugar. Beat together the eggs and milk and stir into the flour along with the cream of tartar and the vanilla extract. Beat to a smooth, thick batter, or use a food processor if you

prefer. Cover and leave to stand in a cool place, or cover and refrigerate until required.

2 Before cooking, beat the mixture again. Heat a lightly greased heavy-based frying pan or griddle and drop dessertspoonfuls of the batter (from the pointed end of the spoon), spaced well apart, onto the pan. Cook fast until bubbles appear on the surface and the undersides are golden.

3 Carefully turn the scones over with a palette knife and cook until golden. Serve as soon as they are cooked with clotted cream or crème fraiche and a fruit conserve, or lightly buttered with honey.

Tip:
This batter keeps well in the fridge overnight, so you can be ready with a treat for breakfast. The scones also freeze well, layered between sheets of greaseproof paper, and quickly reheated before serving.

INDEX